LOCAL
BUSINESSES

RECEIVED

JUL - 6 1995

MSU - LIBRARY

The Nearby History Series
David E. Kyvig, *Series Editor*
Myron A. Marty, *Consulting Editor*

Nearby History: Exploring the Past Around You
by Kyvig and Marty (1982)

VOLUME 1
Local Schools
by Ronald E. Butchart (1986)

VOLUME 2
Houses and Homes
by Barbara J. Howe, Dolores A. Fleming,
Emory L. Kemp, and Ruth Ann Overbeck (1987)

VOLUME 3
Public Places
by Gerald A. Danzer (1987)

VOLUME 4
Places of Worship
by James P. Wind (1990)

VOLUME 5
Local Businesses
by K. Austin Kerr, Amos J. Loveday, and
Mansel G. Blackford (1990)

Local Businesses

Exploring Their History

K. Austin Kerr, Amos J. Loveday, and Mansel G. Blackford

American Association for State and Local History
Nashville, Tennessee

HD
2785
.K43
1990

Copyright © 1990 by the American Association for State and Local History.

All rights reserved. Printed in the United States of America. Except for brief quotations used in critical articles or reviews, no part of this publication may be reproduced or transmitted in any form by any means, electronic or mechanical, including photocopying, recording, or any information storage-and-retrieval system, without permission in writing from the copyright owner. For information, write the American Association for State and Local History, 172 Second Avenue North, Suite 202, Nashville, Tennessee 37201.

Published by the American Association for State and Local History, an international non-profit membership organization. For membership information, please contact Director of Membership Services, (615) 255-2971.

Library of Congress Cataloging-in-Publication Data

Kerr, K. Austin (Kathel Austin)
    Local businesses : exploring their history / K. Austin Kerr, Amos
J. Loveday, Mansel G. Blackford.
        p.   cm. — (The Nearby history series ; 5)
    Includes bibliographical references and index.
    ISBN 0-942063-09-0
    1. Corporations—United States—Historiography.   2. Business
enterprises—United States—Historiography.   3. Local history.
4. United States—History, Local—Handbooks, manuals, etc.
I. Loveday, Amos J.   II. Blackford, Mansel G., 1944–
III. Title.   IV. Series.
HD2785.K43   1990
338.7'4'072073—dc20   90-944
                                                   CIP

Contents

Editors' Introduction

INDIVIDUALS, FAMILIES, LOCAL ORGANIZATIONS AND institutions, and communities instinctively know that their own history is important to them. If they can recall nothing of that past, they are in the same position as people suffering from amnesia, unable to remember from where they came, how they responded to needs or challenges, what produced successes or setbacks, from whence they drew affection and support, or opposition, and where they intended to go. History, much like memory, helps identify familiar elements in new situations, provides a guide to appropriate behavior, and offers a standard of comparison across time and circumstance. In this sense, history is far more than a remembrance of things past, though it certainly includes that. History represents a means of coming to terms with the present, developing an awareness of previous influences, the continuities and distinctiveness in current conditions, and the range of future possibilities. Just as memory helps the individual avoid repeating the same discoveries, behaviors, and mistakes, historical knowledge helps an individual, group, organization, or community avoid starting at the beginning each time an issue needs to be addressed.

The value of historical understanding of the nearby world equals that of national and international history. English historian H. P. R. Finberg considered "the family, the local community, the national state, and the supranational society as a series of concentric circles." He observed, "Each requires to be studied with constant reference to the one outside it; but the inner rings are not the less perfect circles for being wholly surrounded and enclosed by the outer." Indeed, there is great utility in knowledge of the past of the world close at hand, for it is this history that shapes the circumstances we must deal with directly and constantly.

Even if the value of historical understanding is obvious, the means of acquiring it are usually less evident, especially when the subject of interest is local, previously unexplored, and of concern primarily to a small population. Most of us have gained most of our knowledge of the past from books, teachers, museums, films, or other presentations. What is one to do if the subject has never been explored, if there is no book on the topic in the library, if there is no expert to whom to turn? What is to be done in the even more likely circumstance that answers obtained from such sources are insufficient or unsatisfying? The prospect of undertaking original historical research oneself is understandably daunting.

The Nearby History series is based on the premise that history is not only useful, but is also accessible. Any literate person motivated to explore some question regarding the past of his or her immediate surroundings, can master most historical research techniques, pursue most research possibilities, critically evaluate most potential explanations, and achieve a considerable measure of understanding.

In 1982, we wrote a book that asserted the importance of taking a look at the history of the close-at-hand world and attempted to assist readers in doing so. *Nearby History: Exploring the Past around You* was merely an introduction to a broad and complex topic. The book sought to raise questions for consideration, to point out the sorts of materials that exist for historical research, to suggest generally how they might be used, and to indicate some of the published work on nearby historical topics that might offer useful models or comparisons. *Nearby History* was predicated on the belief that useful inquiry into the nearby past was not an undertaking for academic professionals alone, but could be pursued in a worthwhile fashion by any interested student or out-of-school adult. The warm reception which greeted *Nearby History* encouraged us to carry this notion further by providing specific advice on exploring particular topics. The Nearby History series has thus far considered schools, homes, public places, and places of worship; now in volume five the series turns its attention to the important topic of local businesses.

Local Businesses: Exploring Their History by K. Austin Kerr, Amos J. Loveday, and Mansel G. Blackford is a significant addition to the Nearby History series. Kerr and Blackford are professors of business history at Ohio State University and creators of an extraordinarily popular course in American business history for undergraduate business students at Ohio State. Loveday is chief curator of the Ohio Historical Society's history museum. Drawing on their great and diverse experience in researching, writing, teaching, and exhibiting the history of individual businesses as well as American business in general, Kerr, Loveday, and Blackford have created a guide to the investigation of business history that both addresses large issues in a thoughtful fashion and offers a wealth of specific, practical advice.

Anyone considering an investigation of a business's past, especially someone concerned with the ongoing welfare of that business, must first address the issue of the benefits and liabilities of such a study. Kerr and his colleagues outline clearly how important it is for a business to have a full understanding of its own past. Furthermore, they indicate that the larger community can profit from an appreciation of the experience of local business. The authors set forth, for the benefit of those who must decide whether to allow and support business history projects as well as those who conduct them, the questions and issues which ought to be addressed if a business history is to fulfill its potential. Likewise, they explain the types of materials to which the historian needs access in order to achieve worthwhile results. Thus, *Local Businesses: Exploring Their History* equips anyone who might be contemplating a historical inquiry, whether as sponsor, investigator, supporter, evaluator, or simply as user, to judge the merits of such an undertaking.

Austin Kerr, Amos Loveday, and Mansel Blackford clearly hope that a better understanding of sound business history techniques and objectives will encourage libraries and archives as well as businesses themselves to collect and maintain materials for the study of business history. Also, they wish to see such knowledge stimulate additional, more thorough examination of nearby business history by local citizens, historical societies and museums, students, scholars, and by businesses themselves. If so, the goals of the Nearby History series will have been advanced, and the intent of this volume will have been realized.

DAVID E. KYVIG, Series Editor
MYRON A. MARTY, Consulting Editor

Illustrations

THE AUTHORS AND PUBLISHER GRATEFULLY ACKNOWLEDGE the following individuals and organizations for granting permission to reproduce, on the pages listed below, pictorial material from their collections.

Allen County Historical Society (Lima, Ohio), cover, p. 122
Author Collection, pp. 25, 28
Library of Congress, pp. 3, 5, 9, 10, 15, 30, 32, 43, 45, 106
The Nashville Room—Ben West Library (Nashville, Tennessee), p. 120
Ohio Historical Society, pp. 4, 8, 33, 53, 60, 72, 75, 77, 79, 80, 83, 85, 97, 104
Riesbeck's Stores, p. 64

Acknowledgments

IN WRITING THIS BOOK, WE HAVE BENEFITTED FROM MUCH assistance. The librarians of Ohio State University and the Ohio Historical Society have guided us in a most professional way. Special thanks are due to Bernard Block for extraordinary patience in explaining how to locate relevant government documents, and to Robert Thorson who has brought a new professional spirit to historians' work on our campus. David Lincove cheerfully and expertly helped us conduct our first *on-line* computer search for bibliographical information in the field. And George Chalou of the National Archives and Records Administration graciously offered suggestions for improving chapter 5. David Kyvig and Myron Marty, editors of this series, have helped us both to clarify our own goals and to present our material in an understandable way. Funds donated to the business history program at Ohio State University, on whose faculty we serve, helped provide the computers and software that have greatly facilitated our work. Dean G. Micheal Riley and the College of Humanities have provided a small but essential, and much appreciated, grant-in-aid in support of our work. Finally, of course, we alone are responsible for what follows.

Preface

WE DECIDED TO WRITE THIS BOOK IN RECOGNITION OF THE widespread interest in the story of business and of enterprise in the past. As historians of the United States, we have written about the history of business because we acknowledge the central role that the spirit of enterprise, usually expressed through business firms, has played in the history of American politics, society, and culture. Although we do not mean to sing hymns of praise to business entrepreneurs, we believe them, and their firms, worthy of serious study. Entrepreneurs and firms have helped shape the patterns of political, technological, and leisure and work traditions surrounding life in the late twentieth century. We hope that this book will do a small part in helping other persons to appreciate the intellectual rewards of exploring their nearby firms, and we especially want to assist readers in achieving success in such an effort.

More than anything else, we hope that this book is of practical value to the person who is about to launch a study of a local business. By providing practical advice that comes in part from our own experience reading, writing, exhibiting, and teaching business history, we hope to encourage readers to explore the fascinating story of business. Business is an appropriate addition to the Nearby History series that the American Association for State and Local History publishes. For an American, business is always "nearby," and local business—the firm with which we might most commonly associate as a neighbor, employee, customer, or owner—surely deserves careful study.

In providing the steps needed for undertaking a study of a nearby business, we also hope to encourage the effort to take a broad shape. As scholars wanting to understand our nation's past more clearly, we are dissatisfied with histories that are simply worshipful. Such efforts, although sometimes of interest because they can reveal information not otherwise obtainable, do not accomplish all that is possible in enlarging our understanding of the past. Therefore, we have concentrated on the raising of questions, for we believe that is the most useful guidance we can offer. There is no special mystique about historical exploration; we hasten to say, there is no jargon-laden tradition of intricate language to daunt a person who is beginning a history project. Nevertheless, it is certainly of use to have a kind of road map of questions available in order to stimulate thinking about significant matters and to help avoid aimless wandering through historical terrain.

Although our principal interest is in helping our readers develop their own road maps of questions as they begin exploring a local business, we also recognize just how important it is for the traveler to have some idea of how to reach the destination. So this book is full of tips to assist the reader in his or her search for answers to questions. We have provided a few references to the rich literature of American business history, and most especially, references to the guidebooks that all researchers in the field will find so valuable in looking for answers to the types of questions we have raised.

We have made one basic assumption in writing this book: that the reader will be exploring the history of a firm whose origins extend back no further than about 1850. We think our assumption is a correct one, for it is likely that any surviving firm that is older will already have a written history of its activities. In a scholarly sense, moreover, 1850 is also a logical breaking point in the chronology of the firm in America, for by that date a few railroad firms were taking on the shape of the institution we call "big business," an institution that in the second half of the nineteenth century would spread to other industries and profoundly alter the structure of enterprise in American society.

We also should express one caveat at the outset. We wrote this book in part to encourage the study of smaller firms. We welcome new histories of large firms, but especially we are interested in encouraging more work relating the history of the smaller businesses to their communities, states, regions, and nation. Much of this volume, however, arises from our own experience in writing business history; an experience that is necessarily limited, and which is mostly with firms that processed or manufactured goods for sale either to other businesses or to individual consumers and their families. Although the reader may have chosen to study the history of a very different type of firm, say a small retailer or a service business of some sort, we believe the examples that follow offer insight and assistance to the business historian and the task ahead.

LOCAL
BUSINESSES

· 1 ·

Exploring Local Business History

HISTORIANS TELL STORIES, AND BUSINESS HISTORIANS TELL stories about business. "Story," after all, is the core component of the word "history," and we should approach the subject of exploring local business in that spirit. The stories of local business are fascinating, inseparable from stories of the community and often, of the family. In a nation that is so often proud of its business heritage, surely the story of local business is interesting and important because the story enriches knowledge of our national heritage.

All humans feel a need to resort to a historical account in order to bring meaning and clarification to their own experiences. The essence of history is placing topics and analysis in chronological sequence, usually using some sort of a narrative format for explaining what the particular history is about and for explaining the insights gained. Local business history is worthwhile to explore because the task, using the assistance provided in this book along with your own ingenuity, will enlarge your understanding of the community, the family, and, lastly and most importantly, of the firm.

The historical approach is especially attractive for exploring and presenting business because it helps make sense of complicated information and brings new insight by showing how developments, especially human experiences, accumulate and build on one another. This attribute of historical exploration is not only fascinating with regard to the individual business firm, or even entire industries, but also to nearly every other aspect of human experience, however it might be categorized.

With regard to business history, the analogy that David Kyvig and Myron Marty provided in *Nearby History* (their book inspired this one) of

1

concentric circles is an especially useful conception. They described the family, the community, the state, the nation, and the world as a series of concentric circles, each with its own identity but each related to the circles inside and outside itself. Kyvig and Marty suggested the image of concentric circles as a way of bringing added meaning to the study of local history, and it is no less an appropriate image for exploring local business. To understand how the image applies we should consider, at least for a moment, the meaning of the word "business." The word is used to refer to a particular entity, a firm, but an entity that may take very different forms. The individual firm may be in a manufacturing or service business; it may be large, small, or somewhere in between; and it may be a corporation, partnership, or individual proprietorship. This meaning of the term "business" as an individual firm is the starting point for our image, the center of a set of concentric circles.

The term "business" is also, of course, employed in other ways. Americans commonly use the word "business" to mean something broader than the individual firm, such as "the steel business" or "the grocery business." As soon as we think of "business" in this broader sense, we begin to introduce other circles into the concentric rings. Historians exploring local business need to expand their thinking, and the questions they attempt to answer; to encompass a set of rings or circles wider and broader than the particular firm. By doing so they will be able to understand that firm much more clearly and fully. Those rings will vary in scope and size depending, of course, on the type of firm whose history is being explored, and the historical era in which the effort is concentrated. A few years after the Civil War ended in 1865, a local butcher shop was likely to exist in a neighborhood setting. The local butcher interacted with other business men and women and business firms to sell its goods to customers, in a relatively small geographical area; relative, that is, to what would come later with advances in mechanical refrigeration and transportation technologies, and the subsequent rise of giant meat-packing firms that took advantage of those technologies and adapted them in new ways. A steel firm, on the other hand, existed in a set of concentric rings some of which extended well beyond our nation's borders; for the steel business, even in the last decades of the nineteenth century, was international in the scope of its operations.

It is useful to make a distinction in writing and thinking about any exploration in business history between the "firm" and the "industry" (or industries) in which the firm operated. We might all prefer a more precise use

The cotton broker in Memphis in the 1930s was closely connected to an international trading system centered in Chicago.

of our wonderful English language, which would refer to "the steel firm" and to "the steel industry" but never to "the steel business." We do not enjoy such a tidy linguistic environment and tradition, however. The point is not to complain about imprecise language, but to encourage the launching of an exploration in business history in a way that will bring the largest possible meaning to effort. Keeping concentric circles or rings in mind will help the reader meet this challenge.

In the final analysis, we think there are three main reasons for exploring the history of local business: its value (1) to the family, (2) to the community, and (3) to the business firm itself. Here again the notion of concentric rings applies. The image may be becoming too complex, because these rings overlap with the kind of "firm-to-industry" circles, which in a sense are geographical conceptions relating to commercial transactions in the marketplace, alluded to earlier. The history of the firm is worthy of consideration and exploration, and the bulk of this book's attention will be devoted to that aspect of business history, to that set of concentric rings, in the remainder of this chapter and, indeed, this volume. We also wish to emphasize, however, that local business is especially interesting to study because it related, and continues to relate, so closely to the history of the American community and family.

Businesses were often intimately involved in community development in a variety of ways. The Buckeye Steel Castings Company of Columbus, Ohio, financed a reading class for its workers with the Industrial YMCA.

Business and the Community

Investigation of the history of a business will contribute to an understanding of both the specific firm and, more generally, of its locality. The story of each firm takes on meaning when it is understood in terms of the special environments in which business men and women acted. The political, social, and cultural environments of a community impinge upon the firm being studied and need to be explored in order to present a complete picture of the firm's activities. The firm, in turn, has made an impression on the community, and one goal of this book is to clarify some of the ways in which the stories of the business firm and of the community have intersected.

It is difficult to imagine a very complete story of any American community being told without some discussion of how the men and women who lived there in the past, who built and maintained the community, engaged in business. In American society, with the possible exception of a few utopian examples, towns and cities have been established, have existed and prospered, and have died for economic or business reasons. By writing about the development of a firm in its larger contexts, a historian can tell an important story for people who are interested, not just in that particular company, but in the history of the community in general.

There were many types of firms that contributed to the community in which they transacted business. Local historians explore the story of the tiny firm as well as the corporate giant. Within the community the establishment and operation of neighborhoods was impossible without the successful conduct of business. Small shops that serviced retail needs for food,

A small business owner in Minnesota in the 1930s sat at his desk to complete paper work for his firm.

clothing, and recreation were essential. The decline and even disappearance of neighborhoods as communities in which citizens worshiped, worked, and shopped together has been an important part of the life of the American city. After World War II ended in 1945, this decline was closely related to and responsible for the changing climate of economic opportunities that business men and women encountered. Thus, the story, say, of a local pharmacy or butcher shop, is likely to be a tale that was an integral part of the life of a neighborhood community. If the local firm went out of business because of an inability to compete successfully with a large chain store, for instance, it reflected a common and important theme in the history of the community and of the American urban landscape.

In fact, it seems impossible to understand fully the history of any American community without some comprehension of the role of the local real estate business. Even the tiny, one-person real estate brokerage has in its own way affected the shape of the American community. Historically real estate agents channeled customers into particular locations and away from others. Even the smallest real estate firms interacted with their counterparts in shaping their communities. The phenomenon of real estate development, or even of land speculation, stretches well back in American history. {Two of us live in a community (Worthington, Ohio) planned and established in 1803 by a Connecticut real estate developer, James Kilbourne; and one of us lives in a community (Upper Arlington, Ohio) planned as a bedroom suburb at the time of the First World War.} After World War II, real estate developers fashioned shopping malls that have profoundly changed commercial opportunities in numerous American communities even, in some cases, replacing the historic role of the urban department store that emerged in the second half of the nineteenth century.

Even the larger corporation doing business across a region or beyond probably interacted in important ways with the community that housed its offices and plants, with each institution helping to shape the other. In American cities of any size the business leaders have usually played an important civic role. Political and other civic leaders often have looked to business executives for leadership in solving the problems of the community. Corporate executives typically have exercised influence in their communities in visible ways, through a Chamber of Commerce or other local association or service organization. Also they have exercised influence less visibly, through social contacts with one another on the golf course or in the luncheon club, and in quiet meetings with church leaders, journalists, labor union officials, and, of course, politicians. Much has already been written on the influence of business elites in the life of the American community. It is important for the local historian of a business firm to realize that the resulting story will contribute to this dimension of local history.

Finally, a sense of business history will help those interested in local history in general. Business history can provide much of the understanding of how and why communities developed the types of economies they did and how these communities interacted with their neighbors. Those working in or with local and state historical societies will find an understanding of business history especially worthwhile. These historical societies—as well as particular companies—are likely to maintain business records that will be useful in reconstructing community histories.

Business and the Family

Just as the life of a firm occurred within the context of a community's history, so too the history of the firm and of the family often overlapped and intersected, sometimes in ways that were inseparable. Business in America most often was and is personal, and only the largest corporations can really be separated from the institution of the family. A local business most likely will be an integral part of a family's history, and vice versa. This was most often the case in the nineteenth century and, in the twentieth century with the story of small business. Even in the late twentieth century some very large firms, such as Cargill of Minneapolis, Minnesota, are privately held enterprises controlled by the members of a single, if extended, family.

Traditional society, including America before the advent of the industrial revolution of the nineteenth century, saw the development of nearly all business ventures as extensions of family enterprises. In fact, in the American colonies during the eighteenth century the leading firms were known as "houses"; the traditional great merchant houses that engaged in a variety of business ventures disappeared with expanding opportunities for specialized investments of capital in the early national period, but the family nature of business continued. Even as late as the early twentieth century, the nation's leading investment banking firm, J. P. Morgan & Son of 1 Wall Street in New York City, was popularly known as "the House of Morgan," connoting the continued importance of family and business relationships.

Business and family are often inseparable. This 1941 image of a Saturday afternoon in Lancaster, Ohio, demonstrates that nearly every Main Street business was family owned.

The fact that so many firms included "& Son" or "& Sons" in their names was evidence of the continuing importance of family relationships in the organization of business activities in the United States.

Recognition of the important relationships between the history of the firm and the history of the American family will also lead to an understanding of evolving relationships between genders in the history of American society. Exploration of the history of a firm after 1850 involves studying a period of time in which men typically relegated women to subservient roles, at least insofar as commercial activities were concerned. (We know of no firms named ". . . & Daughters.") Gender relationships, however, have changed since 1850. Some employers began a self-conscious policy of hiring women as factory workers during the earliest stages of the industrial revolution, and after 1850 work for women outside the home expanded, first in industrial jobs and, later, in clerical positions. Women always operated some businesses, usually in the retail or service trades; their opportunities for executive or managerial positions and even ownership expanded greatly

In his study of the history of three small businesses in Muncie, Indiana, "Business and the American Family: A Local View," *Indiana
Social Studies Quarterly*, 33 (Autumn 1980): 58-67, the historian
Bruce Geelhoed found the family nature of the businesses to be a
common thread in their success. Geelhoed examined Kirk's, a bicy-
cle and sporting-goods retailer founded in 1865, and by 1980 in its
fifth generation of operation by the Kirk family; the American Lawn
Mower Company, a manufacturing firm started in 1902 and owned
by three generations of the Kersey family; and Riggin's Dairy, a milk
products and agribusiness concern operated by three generations of
the Riggins family. Geelhoed discovered a number of reasons for the
success and longevity of the businesses, but foremost among the
reasons was that the "family orientation of each business undoubt-
edly provided strength in terms of loyalty and identity."

In the early twentieth century, women had entered the clerical work force in large numbers, but were
still usually supervised by men.

Used car dealers had become a noticeable part of the business landscape by the 1930s, as this image of Lancaster, Ohio, indicates.

after passage of the federal civil rights law of 1964, when more women began to assert their rights to equality of economic opportunity.

Looking further at the history of a local firm, the historian needs to remain mindful of the traditional organization of business around family relationships; how business responsibilities are passed down from generation to
generation, usually through the male heirs. That passage, and the intermin-
gled commercial and family tensions that sometimes were involved, was a
significant element not just in the history of the firm and of the family, but
of the community as well. (In fact, that passage has so often been observed
that it is a common theme in American literature.) Furthermore, in the life
of many communities the reduction and even elimination of family ownership, control, and influence in venerable firms was often especially important. A common complaint as early as the 1890s was that the passage from
family, local control of a firm to an "absentee" or nonlocal ownership dam-
aged the well-being of the community that housed the firm. Americans believed then that family and local ownership of a business usually was
accompanied by a sense of stewardship for both the community and the
employees. For instance, in the strike that swept the bituminous coal mining towns of the nation in 1897, sometimes local business leaders helped
the striking miners because both shared a sense of alienation from the mining firms controlled by distant operators. There were officials in state government who complained that absentee ownership by large corporations
had led to worsened, conflict-ridden labor-management relations.

The association of a family name with a business firm remains important
in contemporary metropolitan society, just as so often was the case in the
traditional American small town. The association seems especially important in gaining the confidence of customers for the purpose of enlarging
sales. Business entrepreneurs of many different kinds who are engaged in
dealing directly with the consumer (from real estate broker to used car
dealer) often devote considerable attention and advertising expense to associate the family and the business in the public mind. This phenomenon
gives us a clue as historians to the continuing importance of the associations between business and family history.

Business Reasons for a History of the Firm

There are many reasons for exploring the history of a business firm and
thereby enlarging knowledge of the history of the community, region, and

nation, and perhaps of the family as well. By focusing on the story of the firm as the center of a complex set of concentric rings, the historian can increase insight about the development of a locality. Such efforts can lead to better appreciation of the national heritage. With corporate sponsorship, the stories of individual firms are explored with one of three basic objectives in mind: (1) to provide a tool for the training of management; (2) to provide valuable public relations or advertising material; or (3) to preserve an institutional memory that serves corporate planners.

Businesses sometimes sponsor a history because the executives responsible believe that telling the firm's story to the broader public will serve public relations and advertising goals. American businesses exist in a democratically organized polity that is the ultimate authority over the firm's existence. Public relations activity for American businesses tended to grow as regulatory activity by the government expanded in the twentieth century. It is often to the advantage of a company, thus, to have the public know something of its story and the contributions the firm has made to the larger community. Americans make decisions every day through governmental bodies, voluntary organizations, and labor unions that affect the nation's business firms. Business executives want those decisions to be reached with a full understanding of the complexities of the business world and its history lest the public's actions somehow unjustly penalize the companies and the communities involved. In that sense history can serve the public relations objectives of a business firm quite well.

History sometimes has also served the goals of advertisers. With regard to advertising strategy, older firms making products for sale directly to consumers often have found it to their advantage to have customers associate the firm and its products with a longer tradition. Such historically minded firms recognized that in the popular mind there is an association between venerability and craftsmanship, and therefore with high quality products. Breweries, thus, choose to sponsor the history of their firm and brand name, and use historical images in their advertisements, in an attempt to have beer drinkers think highly of the quality of their product. Because there is a cachet about "the good old days," and a popular respect for the nostalgic, business firms at times will sponsor historical research in an effort to attract customers. We know of one restaurant and bar, for instance, that employed a researcher to provide authentic materials to create the ambience the firm's owners sought.

Peter F. Drucker, a prominent business writer, noted the wisdom of drawing upon experience in reaching important business decisions. In his autobiography, *Adventures of a Bystander* (New York: Harper & Row, 1979) Drucker recounted his experience with Alfred P. Sloan, Jr., who headed the General Motors Corporation for many years and who was so successful as a manager that a business college, the Sloan School of Management of the Massachusetts Institute of Technology, was named after him. In 1943 General Motors had hired Drucker to observe its decision-making processes and to write about its management structure in order to explain them to a new generation of executives who would eventually replace the firm's founders, including Sloan.

Drucker recounted an episode regarding a fiery debate among General Motors' top executives of the automobile giant's accessory division after the war. Two factions argued vigorously, each marshalling facts in support of its position to expand or not to expand accessory production capacity. The group favoring expansion argued that the postwar automobile market would boom and that General Motors would encounter heavy demand from smaller, independent automobile manufacturers for its accessories. After listening to the argument, Sloan charged the executives with testing their position against historical experience. To their surprise, they learned that in the past, when automobile sales had expanded rapidly, the independent automobile manufacturers, instead of purchasing more goods from the industry's giants, had been devoured by larger firms following a merger strategy. Knowledge of this historical experience instructed Sloan and his subordinates to base their investment decisions regarding postwar accessory production on other arguments. Their exploration of historical experience eventually led Sloan and his advisers to decide against enlarging General Motors' capacity to manufacture accessories.

Although the exploration of local businesses will be useful for such purposes, the main use to which a business history is likely to be put is either to provide an institutional memory for a firm or to have motivational and training material available for employees. Developing an institutional memory and training and motivating employees are inseparable. Business executives need to have a sense of their firm's past in order to plan wisely for the future and to make good, carefully considered business decisions;

they should readily ask, "What has our experience been . . . ?" A solid local business history, perhaps by an employee or a retiree, can help the executives answer that essential question.

Knowledge of the history of a firm can help the business executive by lending a valuable perspective to current events. In American business life in recent times, as in other walks of life, the common perception is that the rate of change has accelerated. In this situation, a sense of history can provide a framework in which the strategic planner as well as the business tactician properly can view current events while preparing for the future. What caused the firm to enjoy success no longer may hold in the present or in the future, of course; but historical knowledge of the reasons for a firm's success is essential for evaluating deviations from particular traditions that have served the company well.

One chief executive found that the history of his firm was important for guiding and inspiring future scientific and technological advances. Edward F. Jefferson, who served from 1981 to 1986 as the Chairman and Chief Executive Officer of Du Pont, a leader in the chemical industry, sponsored a history of science and corporate strategy in the twentieth century for that reason. Jefferson noted that America had a society shaped by science and technology, and that science and technology were, more often than not, fostered, organized, and administered by the business firm. For Jefferson, exploring the history of Du Pont inevitably had implications for a very large set of rings surrounding that particular firm. He wrote:

> Those of us who have been part of Du Pont's research tradition realize that it is not enough to say simply that the company invented nylon, neoprene, Teflon, and other products. The scientific work that led to those developments, the organizational approach to the work, and often the resilience and sense of purpose of the scientists and engineers can help guide and inspire research in the future.

Thanks to Jefferson's foresight, future generations of Du Pont executives, scientists, and engineers can evaluate their own efforts more completely.

Investments in preserving the memory of the firm have paid important dividends for some corporations, and not only because history has become for them an important device for planning. Having knowledge of the past is often essential for legal work. History is very useful for instilling an esprit de corps among a firm's employees at whatever level they may serve.

Rural life in America was often closely associated with the entrepreneurial development of agri-business.

Changes in relationships with the government can be understood better in the light of historical experience. Richard Vietor, a professor at the prestigious Harvard Business School, has observed that knowledge of the history of government-business relations in America has aided executives dealing with the phenomena of deregulation that began to sweep through the nation's political and business policies in the 1970s. "You want to understand how the regulations originally affected the segmentation of the market, and what reversing those regulations or removing them will do," he noted. "The historical context helps you see what challenges are being presented now." To facilitate their historical endeavor, an important group of companies has preserved corporate memory with records management programs. At least two hundred American firms now maintain corporate archives, and corporate memories are being used for a range of purposes. Anyone exploring the history of a firm that has seen the value of preserving and managing its historical records is fortunate indeed.

While large companies are most likely to maintain formal archives, a sense of their past can also benefit smaller concerns. Small businesses—those with fewer than five hundred employees or less than $10 million in assets—continue to compose the majority of all businesses in the United States, in fact 99 percent of the total in 1985. In 1982, small businesses accounted for 48 percent of the non-farm employment, 42 percent of the private (nongovernmental) sales, and 38 percent of the gross national product of the United States. And, many of these are family firms. A sense of change and continuity in the past of these businesses can benefit their executives no less than those running big businesses, and for many of the same reasons. An understanding of the history of a small business well may have the bonus of helping to illuminate a family's history.

Opportunities for Preparing a Business History

In thinking about exploring the history of a local business, from whatever motive, it is useful at the outset to evaluate the opportunities. In the chapters that follow we have provided a guide both to the questions that are useful to raise and the ways in which the historian may obtain answers. First, however, it is important to determine whether or not the project can be accomplished. Here we offer some practical considerations for the reader who is contemplating an exploration in local business history. You may be fortunate in having an opportunity to launch your project because the firm you will study is your own, or belongs to an heir or other family members. Or, you may be fortunate in having worked with officers of the firm and having personal relationships with them.

If you are not part of the firm you wish to explore and have not established a relationship with the company's officers or owners, you should try to secure the backing of that firm's top management. Otherwise, you will have to prepare your history from the public record, which, as chapter 5 will indicate, is often rich in materials. (You may, of course, be writing about a defunct firm whose records are held by a public organization such as a state historical society. In such a case, the company's records often will be open for use without any restrictions.) Without the full support of top management you will find it more difficult to prepare your study. Gaining access to corporate documents and arranging interviews with employees may be

A Legal Agreement with Buckeye Steel Castings

The legal agreement between Professor Mansel Blackford and the officers of the Buckeye Steel Castings Company is typical of the types of agreements governing the work of scholars in the field of business history. The agreement was drafted only after several months of "feeling each other out" by Blackford and the executives, and only after a sense of mutual trust had been established. The agreement reads, in part:

First, Blackford will have the final determination of the content and the interpretation of the history. Blackford will be open to suggestions from those at Buckeye on these matters and will allow those at Buckeye to read the first draft of the manuscript history for factual corrections and other suggestions. However, Blackford, not those at Buckeye, will have the final determination over the content and interpretation of the history.

Second, Blackford will be given full access to all company records and papers. The only exception will be matters about proprietary processes and trade secrets. Corporate officers will try in good faith to arrange oral history interviews as requested by Blackford.

Third, the legal ownership of the history manuscript and the notes used in preparing it will be Blackford's, not Buckeye's. Blackford will have the right to publish the manuscript and journal articles based upon it as he sees fit. If Blackford fails to arrange for the publication of the manuscript within two year's of its completion, Buckeye will have the right to publish it or otherwise distribute it as desired.

impossible. Nevertheless, exploring the history of your local firm can still be worthwhile, as the body of "unauthorized" accounts on library shelves will testify. Still, it is a wise strategy to attempt to obtain the support of top management, which may prove to be easy, difficult, or impossible depending on the people and the situations and personalities involved. A great deal of mutual trust will be necessary between you and the company officials, and it may take months to generate that trust and to enlist official support and cooperation. The necessary trust and acceptance may never materialize.

Assuming that you are able to secure support for your project, the next step is to work with company officials in setting up the guidelines determining just how you will conduct your research and do your writing. This can be a very sensitive issue, but facing it avoids misunderstandings and later unhappiness. While an increasing number of business executives are coming to realize the value of the preparation of accurate, unvarnished histories, warts and all, some persons still favor "puff" pieces that present only the most favorable aspects of the firms' past. As outsiders, we have found it best to have written agreements with the companies whose histories we want to prepare before we begin our work. The agreements pledge company officers to open their records to us and help arrange interviews for us. The agreements guarantee our right to research, write, and publish the histories as we see fit without corporate censorship. The agreements give us, not the companies, ownership of our research notes and the resulting manuscript. We agree not to reveal any trade secrets or proprietary processes, and we agree to submit our manuscripts to company officers to review for technical matters (but we, not company officials, determine what constitutes a technical matter). You may wish to have a lawyer help draw up an agreement with the company officers with whom you are working.

In the course of preparing a corporate history, other problems may surface. Business executives frequently do not know what types of historical records their firms possess. For example, when one important manufacturer of mining equipment was approached about its records, the responsible corporate officer pointed to the original charter, hanging on the boardroom wall in a handsome frame, with the claim that it was about all of the historical material remaining. Later, when the manufacturer merged with a large conglomerate, the state historical society received the donation of a treasure of photographs depicting a century-long development of products. Thus, the first task may be to help the firm gather together its historical materials and arrange them into a manageable collection. Then, too, business executives often fail to recognize that usually it is necessary to look beyond their firms for historical documentation about their businesses. As explained in chapter 5 of this book, a wealth of information about companies usually can be found from sources other than the firm's own records.

Once you have decided to explore the story of a local business and have evaluated favorably the opportunities for you to do so, you will have entered the wonderfully exciting world of business history. The chapters that follow will guide you along your way by helping you to raise questions about the firm itself and its intersections with the concentric circles that surround it. They will help you find answers to those questions and, finally, point out some possible ways in which you may want to present the results of your labors to a larger audience. One challenge facing you will be to maintain your motivation and enthusiasm in the face of setbacks and the common problem of discouragement. We hope you do not have that experience, and to help you avoid it we have written the practical advice in the pages that follow to help you avoid discouragement. The suggestions of other readings to which you may turn are intended not only to provide guidance but also to offer inspiration from the work of other business historians.

Suggested Readings

Several studies provide guides to the research and writing accomplished in the field of business history. Henrietta M. Larson, ed., *Guide to Business History: Materials for the Study of American Business History and Suggestions for their Use* (Cambridge: Harvard University Press, 1948), is an annotated bibliography of 4,900 items published by 1948. Robert Lovett, ed., *American Economic and Business History: A Guide to Information Sources* (Detroit: Gale Research Company, 1971), discusses books and articles in economic, business, agricultural, scientific and technological history published between 1948 and 1971. Lance Klass and Susan Kinnell, preparers, *Corporate America: A Historical Bibliography* (Santa Barbara: ABC-Clio Information Services, 1984), presents short abstracts of 1,368 articles in business history published between 1973 and 1982. Thomas Derdak, ed., *International Directory of Company Histories* (Chicago: St. James Press, 1988), lists published company histories.

The Society of American Archivists, *Directory of Business Archives in the United States & Canada* (1980), is a description of all of the corporate archives in the two nations, together with a list of their addresses.

Recent articles have analyzed the value of business history, stressing how it might be used by business executives. Alfred D. Chandler, Jr., "Business History: What Is It About?" *Journal of Contemporary Business*, 10 (Fall 1981): 47-99; Alan Kantrow, ed., "Why History Matters to Managers," *Harvard Business Review*, 64 (January-February 1986): 81-88; Wilbur Kurtz, Jr., "Business Archives in the Corporate Function," *American Records Management Association Quarterly*, 4 (April 1970): 5-11; George Smith and Laurence Steadman, "The Value of Corporate History," *Best of Business*, 4 (Spring 1982): 69-76. "Historians Discover the Pitfalls of Doing the Story of a Firm," *Wall Street Journal*, December 27, 1983, discusses some of the problems business historians have faced in their research and writing. Also interesting are Thomas Cochran, "The Value of Company History: A Review Article," *Business History Review*, 53 (Spring 1979): 79-84; Ralph Hidy, "Business History: A Bibliographic Essay," in Robert Gallman, *Recent Developments in the Study of Business and Economic History* (Greenwich: JAI Press, 1977: 9-15; and Ralph Hidy, "Business History: Present Status and Future Needs," *Business History Review*, 44 (Winter 1970): 483-497.

Finally, several books provide background reading for American business history. Mansel G. Blackford and K. Austin Kerr, *Business Enterprise in American History* (Boston: Houghton Miflin, 1990) is a basic text. Alfred D. Chandler, Jr., has provided the seminal works in the field. His *Strategy and Structure: Chapters in the History of American Industrial Enterprise* (Boston: MIT Press, 1962); *The Visible Hand: The Managerial Revolution in*

American Business (Cambridge: Harvard University Press, 1977) {a Pulitzer prize winner}; and *Scale and Scope: The Dynamics of Industrial Capitalism* (Cambridge, Mass.: Harvard University Press, 1990) should top any reading list in business history. For a superb collection of Chandler's essays, as well as an original essay by the editor, another Pulitzer prize winning business historian, see *The Essential Alfred D. Chandler, Jr.*, Thomas McCraw, ed. (Cambridge: Harvard Business School Press, 1988). The writings of Thomas Cochran are also very important. See especially "The History of a Business Society," *Journal of American History* 54 (June 1967), 5-18, Cochran's presidential address to the Organization of American Historians; *200 Years of American Business* (New York: Basic Books, 1977); and *American Business in the Twentieth Century* (Cambridge: Harvard University Press, 1972).

·2·

Learning the Internal History of a Business

MANY OF THE MOST IMPORTANT QUESTIONS TO BE ASKED and answered in a business history relate to the internal dynamics of how companies develop over time. Understanding how and why a company was founded, how it expanded its operations (or failed to do so), how its management structure and style evolved, and how it interacted with its competitors is crucial. Looking at the impacts that technological changes and alterations in the nature of its workforce may have had upon the business is also valuable. This chapter suggests approaches to researching and writing about the internal development of companies and poses questions to ask about the evolution of the firm under study.

Organizing a History

At the beginning of a research and writing project, it is useful to think about how a history will be organized. The historian needs to consider how to conceptualize the development of the company being studied. Where are the important breaking points in the evolution of the firm? Should the story of the company's growth be told in terms of the generations of the family that managed it (if it was a family firm), in terms of the presidents that ran it, or in some other manner? Writers have approached the preparation of company histories in a number of different fashions.

If a company was dominated by one family throughout its history, it may make sense to organize an account around how succeeding generations ran the firm. Vincent Carosso took this approach in his history of the House of Morgan. A family business, the House of Morgan was shaped by Junius

Morgan and his son, J. P. Morgan, to become America's premier investment banking firm between 1854 and 1913. Carosso divided his book into two parts. The first section dealt with how Junius Morgan founded and built up the company. Within this section topical chapters examine the roles the House of Morgan played in financing government loans and arranging financing for American railroads and industrial corporations. The leadership exercised by Junius Morgan was, it is clear, the cement binding together the firm's increasingly diverse activities. Junius Morgan died in 1890, and leadership of the company passed to his son J. P. Morgan. The second section of Carosso's study, again divided into topical chapters, examines how J. P. Morgan led the firm to national and international dominance in investment banking by the time of his death in 1913. Throughout his book, Carosso combines the generational approach with the topical approach to good effect.

It may make more sense to organize a history around the administrations of a company's presidents, especially if they were forceful people who changed the course of the company's development. Wayne Broehl, Jr., took this approach in his definitive history of John Deere & Company. Surveying this company's history for 150 years, Broehl divided his study into five major parts corresponding to the administrations of the firm's five presidents: John Deere, who founded the company in 1837; Charles Deere, who expanded it in the late nineteenth century; William Butterworth, who consolidated operations in the opening years of the twentieth century; Charles Wiman, who led the company into a new round of expansion between 1928 and 1954; and William Hewitt, who turned Deere into a global corporation in the years 1955 through 1982. Within each section, topical chapters examine such matters as technological change and product development, the production of agricultural implements, labor relations, marketing methods, relations with competitors, and managerial changes.

It may be necessary, however, to take a different approach to the organization of a company's history. If the major events or turning points in a firm's development fail to coincide with generational changes or with changes in presidential administrations, neither of these approaches is likely to prove effective. In their pathbreaking study of the Standard Oil Company between 1882 and 1911, Ralph and Muriel Hidy divided their history into two parts (with the division occurring in 1899), corresponding not to family generations or presidential administrations, but to basic changes in how the company was organized and managed. Within each part topical chapters examine the management of the company, product development, marketing developments, labor relations, relations with governmental bodies, and other matters.

While differing in precisely how they determined the major divisions for their studies, Carosso, Broehl, and the Hidys nonetheless shared a common approach in how they told the stories of their companies' development: they all took a chronological approach. They showed how early events led to later ones. In doing so, however, they soon found that they were telling complex stories. To make those stories intelligible to their readers, they each found it necessary to break down the major chronological divisions of their histories into topical or thematic subdivisions or chapters. Within each major time period, individual chapters investigated how the companies were run, how products were developed and produced, the nature of labor relations, how sales networks were set up, and relations between the companies and the public. This combination of chronological and thematic approaches is often a useful way to present the history of a firm, for it makes complexity manageable.

Approaching the Company's Founding

Once the approach to presenting the firm's history has been decided upon, the next step is to get started on the details of the research and writing. Questions about the formation of the company will probably be the first ones to answer. Who founded the company? What was their motivation? What legal form was chosen for the firm? From what sources did the initial financing come? These are all important questions to address at the outset.

Uncovering who was instrumental in the formation of a company and why they were involved in its origins are important first steps. It may be necessary to delve into the histories of company predecessors to answer this question. Just how did the founders first get to know each other? Were they acquainted through earlier business relationships, family ties, or in some other way? We have found some surprising answers when facing this question in our own work. For instance, some of the backers of an Ohio firm, the Buckeye Steel Castings Company, first became acquainted as members of the Cleveland Gatling Gun Regiment. This quasi-military organization was a group of businessmen formed to drill with two gatling guns in 1878, after a violent nationwide railroad strike in the preceding year—in readiness to maintain law and order in Cleveland should social disruption threaten that city in the future.

In addition to studying how certain people became interested in starting the company, their motivations should be examined as closely as possible. It is likely that more was involved than a simple quest for profits. People forming businesses have done so for a wide variety of reasons, in the past and in the present day. Many nineteenth-century businessmen, especially industrialists, identified closely with their companies, and indeed formed them as a way of doing something they viewed as constructive, something which they thought would benefit their communities. Andrew Carnegie left a profitable career in the buying and selling of stocks and bonds for just this reason. Carnegie entered steelmaking in 1872 because he wanted to create something tangible. Carnegie went on to build the world's largest steel company. Showing his personal identification with his business, Carnegie named its largest blast furnace the "Lucy" furnace after his brother's wife.

A search for adventure and a desire to be their own bosses have also motivated people to start their own businesses throughout American history. A search for a market niche may also have been important to those forming the company. Were the founders developing a new specialty product or service for a new market? An officer of Wakefield Seafoods, a small business set up to pioneer in the catching, processing, and sale of Alaskan king crabs right after World War II, explained that he took part in the founding of the firm because he looked forward "to trying something that had never been done." Despite the long-standing labors of historians and social scientists, not enough is known yet about why people go into business. Your history can contribute to an understanding of the motivations of nascent entrepreneurs.

Why a company's founders chose a certain location for the firm deserves examination. Was it simply that they lived in the area and were familiar with business opportunities in it? Were local labor conditions, tax abatements offered by their communities, and so forth important factors? Were they influenced by connections they had with other businessmen or women in the locality? Or were they, even in their company's earliest years, beginning to look beyond their community? Were they, perhaps, interested in tapping America's national market for their firm's goods or services? As Americans constructed a nationwide system of communications and transportation based upon the telegraph and railroad in the nineteenth century,

While stock certificates do not often contain much information about the operation of the company, their intricate design and rich illustrations may offer the historian images for published or graphic presentations.

transportation advantages led entrepreneurs to favor certain communities as business centers, especially as centers for industry. In the twentieth century, especially in the years since World War II, further advances—trucks, wide-bodied jumbo jets, satellite communications, and so forth—may have influenced the location decisions of the founders of the company.

The legal form that a company initially assumed needs explanation. Was the firm founded as a single-owner proprietorship, a partnership, or a corporation? Was it begun as a franchised operation? Throughout American history, the vast majority of companies have been unincorporated—that is, firms not incorporated under any state laws. Nearly all companies, even the largest ones, formed in colonial times and in the early nineteenth century were unincorporated. Carnegie Steel was organized as a partnership. Businesses were closely held, and there existed little separation between personal and business affairs. Even today most small and many medium-size businesses are partnerships or single-owner proprietorships. However, as companies became larger, especially railroads and industrial ventures, their officers turned increasingly to the legal device of incorporation. In 1811, New York became the first state to enact a general incorporation law, and by the time of the Civil War most industrial states had some sort of general incorporation law. Under the terms of these statutes, as long as company organizers satisfied certain requirements on such matters as the types of officers their companies had and the amounts of paid-in capital they possessed, they could set up their ventures as corporations without having to secure special enabling legislation from the state. By 1904, corporations accounted for some 75 percent of the manufacturing output of American companies.

Businesses organized as corporations possessed two major advantages over unincorporated firms. Corporations had a life of their own under the state laws. When a shareholder died, his or her stock could be sold to someone else, without affecting company affairs. By way of contrast, a partnership had to be dissolved or reorganized whenever one of the partners died or left the business. In addition, by the late nineteenth and early twentieth centuries, state incorporation laws often gave limited liability privileges to investors in corporations. That is, the investors could not be held responsible for the debts of the corporations in which they invested. Partners, on the other hand, were personally responsible for any debts incurred by their businesses. The promise of limited liability served as a strong inducement for investment in corporations, at the very time when companies needed lots of capital to build America's railroads and factories.

A company's legal form may have changed over time, and this would be worth explaining. As businesses expand their activities and need more capital, companies that began their existence as single-owner proprietorships or partnerships often become corporations. An examination of the firm's legal form, in addition to being intrinsically interesting, well may provide insights into how the founders and later leaders viewed their enterprise. Did they see it simply as a vehicle for making money? Or was it an extension of themselves? Understanding the legal form of a company should also help answer questions about how the firm was initially financed.

How was the company financed? By whom? How did the people financing the firm first get to know each other? Was any government aid involved? These are all questions that should be addressed. New, untried companies have not been able to rely upon institutionalized capital markets for funds in America, for investment bankers have been unwilling to handle risky business. For example, as Vincent Carosso has pointed out in his

The experiences of those founding Wakefield Seafoods, a company set up in Seattle right after World War II to catch, process, and sell Alaskan king crab, illustrate the importance of family ties and personal connections in the financing of new small businesses. Lowell Wakefield, an Alaskan and the founder and president of Wakefield Seafoods, was the single largest investor, owning 12 percent of the company's stock. Several major groups provided the rest of the private financing for the company (additional financing came from a forerunner of the Small Business Administration).

All of the groups had some connection to Lowell Wakefield. Wakefield persuaded friends whom he knew from his earlier involvement in the Alaskan herring and salmon industries to invest in his fledgling firm, and these people bought about 10 percent of the company's stock. Wakefield also learned through the Seattle First National Bank, which was providing a commercial loan to his company, of a king crab fishing venture being organized in Tacoma and convinced its members to invest in his company instead. The Tacoma group acquired about 25 percent of the Wakefield stock. Philip Padelford headed yet another set of stockholders, a Seattle group. Padelford heard of Wakefield's proposal from a neighbor who was with a salmon company and, in addition to investing his own funds, convinced a friend, John Hauberg, to buy stock in the new venture. Hauberg, in turn, attracted others from Seattle, most notably several members of the Weyerhauser family, to the company. The Seattle group owned about 20 percent of the stock. Chicago investors owned about an additional 10 percent. Louis Schreiber, an executive with Wrisley Soap, which had its headquarters in Chicago, had become acquainted with Wakefield while serving with the Navy in Alaska during World War II, and after the war he convinced the president of Wrisley Soap and other corporate executives to invest in Wakefield Seafoods.

book on the House of Morgan, J. P. Morgan refused to deal in the securities of General Motors because he thought the company was too risky. Similarly, in the 1980s many companies exploring and expanding the existing boundaries of biological or electronic technologies have complained that investment bankers have ignored their needs for start-up capital.

Typically, new American companies have had to rely instead upon the funds of the founders, their families, and their friends or business

A Wakefield Seafoods fisherman proudly presented the company's product, a giant Alaskan king crab.

acquaintances for their initial capital. Suppliers of equipment may also, in effect, have helped finance them by allowing generous payment provisions. Government may have been involved in the funding of a firm. State and local governments were very active in promoting canals and railroads in the nineteenth century. Set up in 1953, the Small Business Administration has played a significant role in helping bankroll some nascent enterprises in more recent years. Although criticized by some as not going far enough, by 1981 the agency had 500,617 loans totalling $17 billion outstanding to small businesses across the nation.

Questions about the Company

Once the founding of a company has been dealt with, its growth and success need to be explained. (Or, if the company failed, the reasons for its failure need to be analyzed.) How and why did the company grow? What growth strategies did the company's management adopt? Why? How successful were those strategies?

Answers to these questions will probably help illuminate the history of small business in America. As noted in chapter 1, most American businesses are small businesses. Only in those fields where size offers companies advantages, especially economies of scale, have big businesses emerged. In key segments of America's manufacturing economy this has been the case. However, in many other areas—in sales and services, for example—it has not, and small businesses still dominate those fields. Despite the odds against their success, Americans continued to organize 1.5 million new businesses each year in the early and mid-1980s, and, with the decline of many large companies in America's basic industries such as steel and automobiles, small businesses became the most dynamic element in the American economy in the 1970s and 1980s.

In fact, all but 1 percent of America's businesses are small businesses. Of these 13.2 million firms in 1981, 27 percent were family farms, 27 percent were in service industries, and 25 percent were in retailing, with the remainder in other areas. Some 1.5 million of the small businesses were organized as partnerships, another 2.8 million as corporations, and 9.75 million as single-owner proprietorships. Small businesses accounted for 47 percent of the employment in the private sector of the American economy, and, of the 9.5 million new jobs created in America between 1969 and 1976, some 7.4 million were in small businesses.

The smaller firm has historically been an integral part of America's business system.

Nonetheless, small businesses, especially newly formed ones, are risky businesses. Most new companies in the United States have lasted as independent enterprises for only a few years. A majority have either failed, voluntarily dissolved, or been taken over by other companies within just four or five years of their founding. Relatively few have grown up to become mature businesses in their own right. Many reasons have accounted for the difficulties new companies have faced in America, but a lack of adequate financing and managerial expertise seem to stand out. Not enough is known, however, about why companies have failed in times past, for historians have concentrated their efforts on successful firms.

While much also remains to be learned about the factors leading to success in business, more is now understood than just a few years ago. It is rare for a single factor to account for the success or failure of a fledgling firm in any time period. Rather, a set of interrelated elements seems to be significant. Within the firm, the nature of the company's management has been of prime importance and should be investigated. Was management innovative, responsive to technological and market changes? Were the company's managers persistent, willing and able to stick it out in hard times? Perhaps most importantly, did the firm's management have the personal ties to others—financiers, suppliers, and government officials—useful in helping their company over rough spots in its early development? A company one of us has studied was in default on a loan granted it by a forerunner of the Small Business Administration, but the agency gave the company an extension on the loan in part because of personal ties. The regional head of the government agency and the president of the company had been fraternity brothers in college and knew each other well.

Beyond the firm, were the political, social, and market environments favorable to survival and growth? Almost any company, no matter how well run, would have had difficulties starting operations in the depression years of the 1890s or 1930s. Being at the right place at the right time may be crucial to a firm's early success. It is necessary, as well, to look into the relationship between a firm and its competitors in explaining its development. How did the firm relate to its market? It appears that for new manufacturing ventures, in particular, it is important to develop a market niche for products. That is, manufacturers need to develop specialty products or take over special markets ignored by big businesses. Was the firm being studied able to carve out a market niche for its products or services? How did it differentiate them from those of its competitors?

With the initial success of a company established, its expansion should be examined. Did the firm's management limit the company's operations to just one or two major products and markets? Such a growth strategy was common for most American companies, large and small, up to the time of World War I. Even the big businesses that first developed in America between 1850 and 1920 produced only a few goods for a few markets. Or, did the company being studied diversify in terms of its product offerings and the markets it served? As America developed a consumer society in the years after World War I, an increasing number of big businesses diversified. General Electric and Westinghouse, for example, moved from making electrical generating equipment into the production of a wide range of electrical appliances for consumers—electric stoves, refrigerators, irons, and so forth. Since World War II, diversification has become the most common growth strategy of businesses in the United States, as Americans have continued to develop a consumer society dependent upon an outpouring of a plethora of goods and services from their nation's businesses.

This development of big businesses in America in the nineteenth century and their diversification in the twentieth have been investigated quite thoroughly by business historians, especially Alfred D. Chandler, Jr. His

The development of big business in America was closely related to both the railroad and to manufacturing.

books are essential reading for anyone doing research and writing in business history. Particularly worth a careful reading is his *The Visible Hand: The Managerial Revolution in American Business*. In this study Chandler provides a framework within which to view the development of business firms in the United States. Chandler shows how the development of a national market combined with technological breakthroughs in manufacturing to bring about the rise of big business in late-nineteenth-century America. He also investigates how and why these big businesses diversified as they matured in the twentieth century. Chandler's *Strategy and Structure* was also pathbreaking, for it carefully explained how industrial firms adjusted their organizational structures according to their business strategies.

Technological change was often an important part of early twentieth-century business development in America. This photograph, of a ladle used in the steel-casting business, illustrates a new way of lining with cement instead of brick.

Some companies have followed growth strategies that have taken them beyond the United States to become multinational enterprises. Multinationals have long existed in American history, as a wide range of reasons have lured United States firms overseas, but an increasing number have engaged in foreign activities since World War II. By 1970, at least 3,500 American companies had direct foreign investments in some 15,000 enterprises. Even some family firms such as the Norton Company of New England have become multinationals. Did the company under investigation become a multinational? If so, how and why?

Whether studying small or large firms, many historians have been stressing the importance of understanding interactions between technological and business changes. These connections are well worth exploring. In fact, as Glenn Porter, a business historian who heads the Hagley Museum, a major center for research in business history, has observed, the history of business and the history of technology are becoming intertwined evermore.

How have technological changes affected the company being examined? Did they lead to the development of new products? Did they affect company structure?

> The connections between technological change and corporate growth have been probed in detail by the business historian George David Smith in his *From Monopoly to Competition: The Transformation of Alcoa, 1888-1986* (New York: Cambridge University Press, 1988). From the first, Smith shows, Alcoa was driven by its technological innovations to develop new markets for its products. How Alcoa succeeded in opening markets at home and abroad, and how these efforts, in turn, shaped the style and structure of the company's management form a fascinating story. Particularly valuable is Smith's analysis of the establishment in 1928 of a research laboratory by Alcoa and the subsequent work of that facility. By World War II Alcoa had become one of America's most successful monopolies. After the war new considerations, including technological ones, reshaped the American aluminum industry into an oligopolistic one, an industry dominated by three large firms—Kaiser and Reynolds, in addition to Alcoa.

By the same token, it is important to consider how changes in a company's workforce may have affected that company's operations. How did the firm recruit, train, and manage its workforce? What was the composition of the workforce? Did the company engage in "welfare capitalism," the provision of housing, recreational, and medical services for its workers? If so, why? Was it to build up worker loyalty to the company, thus cutting down on the turnover rate, the proportion of workers leaving the company each year? Was the company union or non-union? Did the company oppose or accept unionization? Did a "corporate culture," a way of thinking and acting, develop to unify managers and workers? Did considerations about their relations with their workers affect managerial decisions by the company's officers? Did any of these considerations change over time?

Finally, whether it is a small or large company being investigated, the business may well have been involved in a merger at some point in its history, for merger waves have periodically reshaped the business scene in the United States. Four merger movements have been of particular importance.

The first, lasting from about 1895 to 1904, witnessed the creation of many of the first big businesses in American history, the formation of United States Steel in 1901, for example. The second, which took place between 1925 and 1931, saw an additional concentration in American industry, as nearly 6000 mergers occurred. The third, taking place in the 1960s, saw the creation of conglomerates, firms engaged in a wide range of unrelated activities. Finally, a new merger movement beginning in the mid-1970s and lasting into the late 1980s has been altering further the business world.

Many questions might be asked about a company's merger experience. Most fundamental, however, are those of motivation. Why did the merger take place? Was the company seeking a merger? If so, why? Or, was the company the target of an acquiring firm? What type of merger was it? Friendly or unfriendly? Finally, it is important to try to determine the results of the merger. Did it alter the company's operations? Did it lead to managerial changes? Only by understanding mergers and their results can we fully comprehend the nature of modern American business.

Asking Questions about a Firm's Management

With the development of a company's operations well established, how its management evolved over time is to be considered next. How did managerial changes relate to alterations in the company's operations? As the scope and complexity of the firm's operations increased, did the nature of its management change?

Of course, the company being studied may have experienced little change in its type of management. Most new companies begin with a personal management set-up, a situation in which company officers know each other well as friends and work together informally. In small companies there may be little separation of ownership from management, as company officers often invest heavily in their enterprises to get them on their feet. Officers may also know their workers personally, and may indeed fill in on production lines themselves when needed. Nearly all American businesses were small businesses run by informal, personal management systems up to the mid-nineteenth century. This type of informal, personal management persists in small businesses to the present day. If a company offers only a limited number of goods and services for a few markets, personal management based upon mutual trust between the top officers may suffice.

In such a situation family ties may be of importance. These are worth investigating, for not enough is known about the continuing significance of family connections and traditions in the shaping of company policies. It appears that families, either overtly or covertly, develop and enforce their own traditions and values in family-controlled business firms. Even some large businesses such as Hewlett-Packard, Wrigley, Marriott, and Hallmark are imbued with family values. Hewlett-Packard, for example, has until very recently treated its employees as an extended family, refusing to fire anyone even in times of economic downturn.

However, as big businesses developed in America—first in railroads from the 1840s on, and a bit later in some industrial fields from the 1880s on—personal, informal management gave way to bureaucratic management in many firms. As companies became larger and more complex in their operations, it became impossible for a handful of people at the top to provide them with adequate management. Particularly important in shaping changes in the management structures of companies was the development of new markets and new products, for these developments greatly increased the complexity of the operations of the firms. It was the increase in the complexity of their operations more than any sheer increase in their size that led many big businesses to shift from personal, informal management to impersonal, bureaucratic management.

The development of bureaucratic management encompassed major changes in how companies were run. There was, first of all, a separation of ownership from management. As an increasing proportion of firms became corporations and stock ownership became dispersed, salaried managers, who often had little of their own money invested in the corporation, came to run big businesses. Then, too, for the first time, middle management developed, for no longer could members of top management adequately control their companies' complex affairs by themselves. While a firm's top managers made the big policy decisions for their company's future and coordinated the work of its different parts, the company's middle managers made the operating decisions on how to turn out its products. Historians need to know more about the development of middle management, and your history may well contribute to the understanding of this topic. Finally, business leaders developed a flow of financial information up and down the line of authority from top to middle management to hold together the complex operations of their companies. Particularly important was the development of sophisticated cost, capital, and financial accounting.

The spread of bureaucratic management generally occurred in two stages.

In the mid- and late nineteenth century some railroads and leading industrial firms developed strong central offices, what historians often call "centralized" management. Committees of top managers ran the different functions of the firms. By 1886, for example, the Standard Oil Company had committees responsible for such functions as transportation, refining, and sales. As the operations of big businesses became more complex in the twentieth century, however, centralized management systems often broke down. They could not handle the increased number of products and markets in which firms became involved. Led by Du Pont and General Motors, a growing proportion of big businesses since World War I have replaced centralized management with what is usually called "decentralized" management. In decentralized management systems, companies are usually organized around product divisions, such as the Chevrolet Division at General Motors. These divisions design, manufacture, and sell their companies' products. They are run by division superintendents, middle managers who make the operating decisions for their firms. Coordinating the work of the divisions and planning for the future of their companies is top management, the officers who make the strategic decisions for their firms. By 1970, about 86 percent of the five hundred largest industrial companies in America possessed at least three major divisions, and most of these firms were being run by decentralized management systems.

In examining a firm's history, it is important to ask whether or not the company's management underwent an evolution from personal to bureaucratic arrangements. A key concern to keep in mind is the relationship between the nature of a company's management and the scope of its operations. The growth strategy a company pursues is likely to influence strongly the type of management it has. The more diverse a company's products and markets, the more likely it is to be run by some form of decentralized management. Did decisions to produce new products and enter new markets affect the management of the company? And, if it did, why and how did the changes occur? Were they related to an increase in the complexity of the firm's markets and products?

There are additional questions to ask about the management of the company whose history is being prepared. Most important are those of motivation. As the company grew and, perhaps, developed a bureaucratic management system, did the motivation of its managers change? It did, for instance, at General Motors. Billy Durant founded and built up the company as a daring entrepreneur. He ran the company as a one-man show, and for him growth was the major goal. However, Durant failed to provide an adequate management system for General Motors, bringing the firm close to bankruptcy in the early 1920s. Forced out of General Motors, Durant was replaced by Alfred P. Sloan, Jr. More of an organizer than Durant, Sloan established bureaucratic management at General Motors. With this change, increasing returns on investments became more of a goal than growth for growth's sake.

Beyond questions of motivation are those concerning sources of leadership. It is wise to examine the social and economic backgrounds, including the education, of the businessmen and businesswomen being studied. And, their career paths should be investigated. Did members of top management work their way up from within or were they recruited from outside the company? What impact did their career paths have upon the company? For example, were their backgrounds related to how innovative or responsive the company was in initiating or responding to technological or market changes? Did their backgrounds contribute to the development of a corporate culture, certain values and ways of doing things shared by most people in the company?

Conclusion

There are, then, many questions to ask about the internal dynamics of a company's development, especially about the relationship between changes in its activities and its management. These questions will, in turn, lead to inquiries about a company's relationship to its social and political environments. As the company grew, did its position in its community change? Did its stance with regard to political bodies and governmental agencies change? These are the types of questions raised in the next chapter.

Suggested Readings

Collections of case studies explore the development of the business firm in America. Alfred D. Chandler, Jr., and Richard Tedlow, eds., *The Coming of American Capitalism: A Casebook on the History of Economic Institutions* (Homewood: Richard Irwin, Inc., 1985), presents thirty cases from Benjamin Franklin to General Electric in 1981. Henry Dethloff and C. Joseph Pusateri, eds., *American Business History: Case Studies* (Arlington Heights: Harlan Davidson, 1987), presents fifteen cases. Richard Tedlow and Richard John, Jr., eds., *Managing Big Business* (Boston: Harvard Business School Press, 1986), reprints fourteen articles on the history of the business firm that first appeared in the *Business History Review*. Several studies, in addition to those authored by Alfred D. Chandler, Jr., and cited at the end of chapter 1, are especially valuable for an understanding of how big businesses with bureaucratic management systems developed in the United States. Glenn Porter and Harold Livesay, *Merchants and Manufacturers: Studies in the Changing Structure of Nineteenth-Century Marketing* (Baltimore: Johns Hopkins University Press, 1971), stresses the impact of market changes on the firm. Vincent Carosso, *The Morgans: Private International Bankers, 1854-1913* (Cambridge: Harvard University Press, 1987), examines investment banking and its role in financing the development of big business. Ralph W. Hidy and Muriel E. Hidy, *Pioneering in Big Business, 1882-1911* (New York: Harper & Brothers, 1955), looks at the development of Standard Oil, and Wayne G. Broehle, Jr., *John Deere & His Company and Its Times* (New York: Doubleday, 1984), examines the evolution of Deere over 150 years.

On the overall development of American multinationals see Mira Wilkins, *The Emergence of Multinational Enterprise Abroad from the Colonial Era to 1914* (Cambridge: Harvard University Press, 1970), and Wilkins, *The Maturing of Multinational Enterprise: American Business Abroad from 1914 to 1970* (Cambridge: Harvard University Press, 1974). The essays comprising Alice Teichova, Maurice Levy-Leboyer, and Helga Nussbaum, eds., *Multinational Enterprise in Historical Perspective* (Cambridge: Harvard University Press, 1986), are also valuable. Charles W. Cheape, *Family Firm to Modern Multinational: Norton Company* (Cambridge: Harvard University Press, 1985), is an excellent case study.

A growing number of studies are available on small businesses. The essays in Stuart Bruchey, ed., *Small Business in American Life* (New York: Columbia University Press, 1980), present an overview of the development of small business throughout American history. Mansel Blackford, *Pioneering a Modern Small Business: Wakefield Seafoods and the Alaskan Frontier* (Greenwich: JAI Press, 1979); Blackford, *A Portrait Cast in Steel: Buckeye International and Columbus, Ohio, 1881-1980* (Westport: Greenwood Press, 1982); and Amos Loveday, *The Rise and Decline of the American Cut Nail Industry* (Westport: Greenwood Press, 1983), present case histories in the historical development of small businesses. The summer, 1989, edition of the *Business History Review* is devoted to the history of real estate. Steven Soloman, *Small Business USA: The Role of Small Companies in Sparking America's Economic Transformation* (New York: Crown Publishers, 1986), is an excellent survey of changes occurring in small businesses in the mid-1980s. David Storey, ed., *The Small Firm: An International Survey* (St. Martin's Press, 1983), places those changes in international perspective.

The relationships between businessmen and businesswomen, their environments, and their communities are explored in many studies. James Williard Hurst, *The Legitimacy of the Corporation* (Charlottesville: The University Press of Virginia, 1970), examines the changing legal environment of business. Daniel Nelson, *Managers and Workers* (Madison: University of Wisconsin Press, 1975), and Robert Ozanne, *A Century of Labor–Management Relations at McCormick and International Harvester* (Madison: University of Wisconsin, 1967), investigate labor relations. William Whyte, Jr., *The Organization Man* (New York: Simon and Schuster, 1956), and Michael Maccoby, *The Gamesman*, (New York: Simon and Schuster, 1976), provide insights into the character of modern businessmen and businesswomen.

·3·

Developing the History of a Business
in its Environment

EXPLORING THE HISTORY OF THE LOCAL BUSINESS FIRM IN its larger context, the environment in which business was conducted, is very important. Understanding the local firm can do so much to enlarge our knowledge of the community in general. Historians are always looking for ways to bring out the meaning of their work, to make greater sense out of the information they have observed. There is no better way to bring out meaning than to find the relationships between the particular case under study and other institutions and external influences.

This chapter will look at some of the most significant considerations regarding the firm as the center of the series of circles suggested as a useful conception in chapter 1. Although those circles may overlap rather than provide an ordered set of concentric rings, they nevertheless represent important areas of inquiry for the business historian. We need to inquire about the firm in its community setting, as it relates to the people around it as a source of employment and as a citizen among other citizens. Similarly, we need to explore the firm in its governmental setting, at the local, state, and federal levels. Overarching all of those considerations, we need to understand the firm in the context of its market setting. It is this last area of business and its environment that is perhaps of most importance to the historian. No firm can exist in a vacuum, and in a free enterprise system the market environment is a sort of engine that powers any firm.

The historian must not be led astray by the notion of *free enterprise*, however. On the one hand, free enterprise developed during the twentieth century as a phrase of powerful symbolic value. Sometimes the rhetoric about free enterprise suggested that business should operate independently of government and other American institutions. Americans are, of course, free to accept the political beliefs that free enterprise connotes, but as analysts we are ill served if we accept those beliefs as truisms about the independence of business. However much we may hold dear the notion of the *rugged individual*, as historians we will miss too much that is significant in our community's history if we try to consider the firm apart from other American institutions, and the business executive as a person without a complex personality.

The idea of *free enterprise*, on the other hand, indicates the importance of knowing something of the larger historical forces that impinged upon the firm under scrutiny. The market, that invisible set of impersonal economic forces that creates opportunities for business enterprise, is the most important of those larger forces for the business historian. But it is worthwhile to be aware of other factors as well, keeping in mind a general knowledge of the reshaping of American history over the years. For example, during the twentieth century Americans chose the automobile as their preferred transportation device, and even if the firm under study is not directly related to rising automobile use, there is a good chance that this *historical force* affected the company's history in some important ways. Those ways may have included the ability to recruit employees or the very location of the firm—from Main Street to the shopping mall.

Business and the Environment of the Market

Each firm has a particular market that constitutes an essential part of the environment the business historian needs to explore. To express the concept in economists' terms, the market represents the demand side of an equation—the goods and services that other firms or people want—while the firm under study represents the supply side—the provider of goods and services. Relationships between supply and demand lie at the core of economics, and likewise relationships between market and firm exist at the center of the business historian's concerns. Business historians recognize the combination of market, government policies, available labor force, and technologies that provides the opportunity for entrepreneurial activity.

Somewhere in the earliest stages of exploring the local firm the business historian must ask the question, what market is the firm trying to satisfy? This question appeared in another form in the last chapter, in the discussion of strategy and structure. Every firm has a strategy, and that strategy,

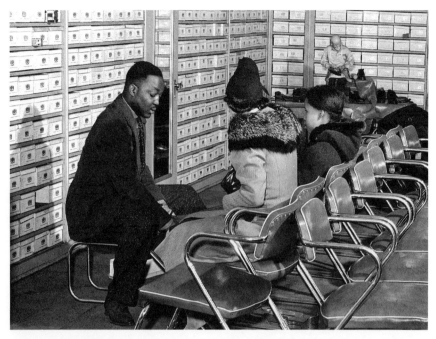

Sometimes a small firm developed to satisfy a particular market niche, as this image of a local shoe store in a black community indicates.

whether implicitly or explicitly, is defined and developed in terms of potential customers and what they desire. It is important to understand the market environment as a major element in shaping the firm's strategy.

The broad changes in market opportunities throughout American history provide a framework for understanding the business firm. Those developments in market opportunities have a lot to do with changing transportation technologies and with the enlarging wealth of the American people. During the nineteenth and even the early twentieth centuries the emphasis in American culture was on production, on building a material society for future generations. Nineteenth-century Americans built entire manufacturing and transportation industries, like steel and railroads, whose main markets consisted of providing goods and services to other businesses. As the nation grew wealthier, however, America became a "consumer society" in which larger and larger numbers of people provided a demand for the conveniences and amenities of life. After about

1920—the phenomenon defies precise dating—the dominant orientation of Americans was as consumers, not as producers, and business opportunities underwent a metamorphosis accordingly.

This changing market context has major implications for the history of local businesses. Keep in mind the market context when examining a firm's strategy, and how that strategy evolved. Was the firm primarily providing goods and services for other firms? That is, were its markets other businesses? Or, was the firm trying to reach individual consumers directly? Was it involved in a mixture of the two functions? What sort of continuity or change was occurring? If the nearby business was providing something to other firms, was its market primarily one that was consumer oriented? For instance, the advertising business was just beginning to appear in the late nineteenth century, but as advertising flourished in the 1920s, the business was very much a part of "the consumer society," even though the typical advertising agency had business transactions with other firms.

The geographical scope of the market has had a profound impact on the development of the American business firm. From 1789, the United States was a nation of continental proportions that provided a large "free trade zone" for economic exchanges largely uninhibited by tariffs or other legal barriers. Nevertheless, the size of the market for most firms remained small and local until the latter part of the nineteenth century. Then, as the population grew in the nineteenth century, reaching nearly 63 million persons by 1890, and as cities mushroomed and were connected by reliable railroads, the scope of the market for more and more firms became regional and even national. It was this change in the market that helped account for the rise of "big business." Entrepreneurs developed distribution systems stretching across huge areas and reaching large numbers of potential customers, and then developed large-scale production systems to supply those same customers.

While exploring the history of a nearby firm, the historian needs to ask a geographical question about the kind of market that the company was in. Was the market local, regional, national, or international? Did that definition of the market change over time? It is wise to remain alert to the developing technologies of transportation and distribution that changed the market. How did the firm adapt to those changes? Raising those questions enables the historian to consider the kind of competitive environment the firm faced. For instance, a butcher in a city at the end of the civil war experienced very little competition because the available technologies for transporting and distributing fresh meat required the supplying firm to be close to its retail customers. But within a generation, the development of mechanical refrigeration and high-speed refrigerated railroad trains meant that the local butcher faced competition from large meat packers located in Chicago. Similarly, the introduction of wide-bodied jet cargo airplanes after 1970 sometimes meant that American manufacturers lost the advantage of proximity in supplying high-value electronic parts in a timely way to customers and faced unprecedented competition from foreign producers.

The dynamic qualities of the market and of the competitive struggle to satisfy market demands provide an essential structure of the business environment. Understanding the changing geographical nature of the market can be especially useful to the local historians, but it is not the only significant way to conceptualize the market. Modern day business executives often think in terms of segmentation when they consider the market, dividing the market into groups or types of people, such as women or men, youth or senior citizens, or the wealthy or *up-scale* customer (the term "up-scale," of course, implies that there are other parts of the market because

This farmer was going from broker to broker to negotiate the best price for his cotton crop in the 1930s.

America does not divide income or wealth equally). Segmentation, or what is sometimes called *market niche*, is a phenomenon often worth exploring. Market niche is especially important in the investigation of the nearby and smaller firm. Niches are like cracks in something bigger, opportunities in the market left open by large, high-volume producers. Smaller firms sometimes prosper because they have established a niche for themselves in the market of their industry. During the 1980s, for instance, while several of the largest steel manufacturing firms in the United States went bankrupt, some so-called *mini-mills* were prospering in part because they were efficiently supplying special kinds of steel products to specialized markets. Was the firm under study successful in establishing a particular niche in the market for itself?

Moreover, in seeking to understand the evolving market setting of a local firm, the business historian also wants to comprehend the competitive situation in which the firm found itself. Competition implies winners and losers. Thus an important question for all business historians is, to what extent has the firm under investigation dominated other firms, or has it been dominated by them?

Business and the Competitive Environment

Although it is really not possible conceptually to separate the market and competitive environments—competition, after all, occurs in a market—the notion of market niche suggests the importance of inquiring about the firm's strategy regarding competition. In the American economy, especially after the advent of cheap transportation in the interior of the nation during the nineteenth century, firms have often had to deal with competition, and their resulting strategies have profoundly shaped their history. The fact that business executives frequently refer to competition is an indication of their awareness of its importance, an awareness that the historian of a nearby firm also needs to maintain. Each firm, consciously or unconsciously, has a strategy regarding its relations with other firms with which it is in competition.

In strategy regarding competition, it was common historically for the entrepreneur to try various means to avoid competition, to bring competition under control if not to eliminate it altogether. Those means included efforts to improve efficiency, to be the low cost, yet still profitable, provider of goods and services. Andrew Carnegie built the world's largest steel company in the nineteenth century, for example, by pursuing cost reductions with a vengeance, so that by the 1890s Carnegie Steel could sell steel profitably at a price below the cost of production of other firms. When exploring a local business, it is useful to look for the firm's strategy of controlling costs.

Efforts to control competition, however, have historically gone well beyond striving for efficiency. Business leaders have in the past engaged in various forms of collusion, now generally against the law, to try to stem competition. Exploring an older firm you may well encounter forms of cooperation not now practiced. Pools and trusts were devices sometimes used to try to control competition in the second half of the nineteenth century. Pools occurred when entrepreneurs agreed to divide a market according to some predetermined arrangement (in other words, when they agreed not to compete). The Iowa Pool in the railroad industry was a famous example, when in 1869 the executives of three railroads, the Burlington, Northwestern, and Rock Island, all linking Chicago with the transcontinental Union Pacific at Omaha, agreed to place their revenue in a common pool. They agreed to keep 45 percent of their passenger revenue and half of their freight revenue to cover their costs, and pooled the balance for equal division among the three carriers. The Iowa pool, like most such arrangements, had a checkered history, partly because the agreement was not enforceable under American law and partly because other railroads wanted either to enter or to disrupt the pool. Trusts were other arrangements designed to eliminate competition. In a trust arrangement, entrepreneurs agreed to turn over control of their firms to a common board of trustees who ensured that each company was operated in concert with others who were part of the arrangement. Trusts were so notorious an arrangement in the latter decades of the nineteenth century that the word "trust" took on a larger meaning, as a synonym for "big business." When Congress enacted the Sherman Antitrust Act in 1890, in effect it meant to have a law against "big business."

Trusts and pools were illegal in federal law after 1890 (some states passed laws banning them before 1890, and judges and juries frowned on them before then also), so business leaders had to turn to other means to control competition. Mergers have sometimes been a response to competition. American law has disapproved of cartel-like arrangements but has been fairly tolerant of combinations among firms. The American business system has periodically experienced waves of mergers between firms. As mentioned in the last chapter, the first great merger wave occurred between

1897 and 1904 when more than 1,800 firms disappeared into consolidations. That great wave of mergers has been followed by others, and a general trend of American business history in the twentieth century has been the concentration of assets into fewer and fewer firms. The historian of the nearby firm often will need to sort out the ownership of the firm under investigation. Was it once independent, then a subsidiary of a larger firm? Was the firm sold and resold more than once? Did the nearby firm acquire other firms? Were the mergers seen as friendly, or were they hostile takeovers?

More often than not a business has tried to have a strategy of coexistence with competition and with competitors, especially regarding prices. Business leaders cannot control competition through cartel-like arrangements, but when objectives are similar, and the information about business conditions is shared among firms, the practical result has often been pricing policies that are remarkably similar. Executives develop similar information, do similar analyses of costs, employ similar technologies, and end up with prices that are similar. Competition in the modern setting of the consumer society has often come in areas like packaging and service. But always there is a possibility of competition, perhaps lurking in the background of the business environment lest a firm become so inefficient that a rival will seize its markets; or perhaps competition is clearly present, as with the situation that developed after about 1970 for so many American manufacturers who had to face, for the first time in memory, vigorous foreign competitors.

Coexistence with competition and competitors may be an important theme in national and community business history, but it was not always the strategy that business entrepreneurs followed. Throughout American history there have been firms that competed aggressively, sometimes by cutting prices. It was a common phenomenon in the history of American business for firms to seek larger shares of a particular market, and once having obtained the desired market share, to have protected the position. Business entrepreneurs are constantly facing the prospect that some change in the business environment may challenge their ingenuity to maintain their position in the market, and even to remain afloat as a viable endeavor. For example, changes in energy costs may have undesirable effects, or another firm may adopt a commercially superior technology with a devastating impact on rivals' competitiveness. The realization of the possibilities of such changes has led business executives to maintain a watchful eye on the business environment and to protect their firm by a strategy of competitiveness.

Trade Associations

While exploring the business environment, you will probably discover that the firm belongs to one or more trade associations. Even a small, family owned retail shop is likely to belong to a Chamber of Commerce or neighborhood commercial association of some kind. Trade associations began to appear in the middle of the nineteenth century, but they proliferated after the turn of the twentieth century. Trade associations brought together firms in the same industry who had common interests, or they were general associations of business, such as a Chamber of Commerce in a particular city. Through the trade association business executives shared experiences, pooled information about costs, prices, sources of supply, and markets. Historically, officials of the federal government have encouraged the formation of trade associations. For instance, the United States Chamber of Commerce formed at a meeting called by President William Howard Taft in 1912. Trade associations were agencies through which government officials acquired and disseminated information about industrial activity, and remain as the most common agency through which public officials and business leaders interact. Trade associations sometimes have engaged in political activity directly, trying to influence the outcome of elections or the legislative process.

The trade association itself may provide an important source of information about a nearby business. Trade associations often published magazines or newsletters, and records of meetings, for their members. For example, the United States Brewers' Association, one of the nation's original trade associations when it formed in 1862, held meetings at which member firms shared insights about the changing technologies of manufacturing and distributing lager beer. Leaders of the industry spoke out on issues of public policy, especially taxation and prohibition legislation, and the Association's historical materials might provide the historian of a local brewery with interesting information.

Thus the historian of a firm will want to inquire about trade association affiliations. To what trade associations did the firm belong? When and for what purposes did the firm join trade associations? What did the firm gain from membership? Did the firm interact with public officials through trade associations? Did the firm's executives play leadership roles in the trade association? And finally the historian of a nearby business, ever alert for reliable and valuable information, will want to ask, what can be learned

Small business owners, no less than big business executives, were active in the formation of trade associations and other forms of business organizations. In his "Small City Industrialists in the Age of Organization," *Business History Review,* 33 (Summer 1959): 178-189, James Soltow, a scholar who specialized in the history of small businesses, discusses how and why small-scale industrialists established the Manufacturers' Association of Montgomery County, Pennsylvania, in 1908, and then traces the development of the organization over a fifty-year period. Using the records of the association and the correspondence of its officers, Soltow shows how the association was formed to fight state legislation deemed harmful to small business, especially new laws proposed to regulate the employment of women and children. The association, however, soon broadened its activities to emphasize the performance of a wide range of services for its members, including the dissemination of the most modern business techniques, such as new accounting practices. An indirect, but highly valued, result of the association's work, Soltow demonstrates, was to elevate the social status of small business persons belonging to the association to something nearer that of big business executives.

from the trade association about the firm and its relationship with other businesses?

The Business Firm and Its Community

Exploring the nearby social environment of a firm is important in order to understand the full texture of its history. Doing so not only enriches historical knowledge of the business but of the local community as well. Businesses typically are more than economic beings. They are also social institutions of owners and employees and citizens of a local community in which they play leadership roles that, strictly speaking, are not profit-seeking. Like everything else about the environment of the firm, its relationships with its community are dynamic, with changes in one affecting changes in the other institution. Exploring the dynamics of those relations will enrich the history of the nearby firm.

Every firm exists in some sort of community and relates to the people of that community as an employer. Those relationships are diverse, of course,

Businesses sometimes sponsored recreational activities for their employees, as part of personnel policies.

but exploring them allows a historian to appreciate the business firm as a human institution. Firms have recruited and trained employees and thereby profoundly altered the lives of individuals, families, and communities. Sometimes firms have recruited employees from distant places, changing the ethnic, religious, and racial population of communities dramatically. Immigrants crowded into industrial areas of the United States before 1924 because of the employment opportunities provided by businesses. So too did rural Americans, both black and white, migrate to cities, providing a constant process of change and renewal both for the employing company and the community of which it was a part.

The personnel policies of a firm are thus well worth investigating. Who worked for the firm? Did the origins of its workers change over time? Did the company employ women as well as men, blacks as well as whites, immigrants as well as those who were native born? How did those patterns evolve, and for what reasons? And especially, what impact did the firm have on the community or communities of which it was a part through its employment practices? Did it try to train, educate, and even control the lives of workers? Did the firm provide opportunities for the disadvantaged to gain desirable skills, immigrants to learn English, for instance?

Business leaders often recognized that what their firms were doing both created opportunities for the community and presented problems to the community. The business firm is a citizen of the community of which it is a part. It is well to be alert to community groups' perceptions of and responses to the problems associated with the nearby firm. (Many firms presented no special problems to the communities, of course.) As manufacturing firms grew, they presented their communities with tasks of providing needed services for the firm and its employees. How did business leaders work together with civic leaders to resolve problems such as providing adequate water and sewer services? Were the business leaders concerned about such matters as housing for their employees? Did they provide leadership in ensuring that families had adequate educational opportunities? What were the self-conceptions of the firm's executives regarding their

The labor historian Gerald Zahavi offers a valuable analysis of the complex interaction between a company, its labor force, and the community in which it was located in his *Workers, Managers, and Welfare Capitalism: The Shoeworkers and Tanners of Endicott Johnson, 1890-1950* (Urbana: University of Illinois Press, 1986). Using records from two dozen factories and tanneries in the region around Binghamton, New York, together with numerous oral history interviews, Zahavi traces management development of welfare capitalism and the workers' responses to it over a sixty-year period. Endicott Johnson established a broad array of welfare practices—profit-sharing plans, medical services, athletic facilities, homebuilding programs, and the like. Designed to keep workers loyal to the company and to discourage the formation of unions, the welfare programs worked. Even during the New Deal, workers largely rejected unionization at Endicott Johnson. However, welfare capitalism succeeded only because it was a genuine two-way street, a compact between management and labor, giving workers much of what they wanted. Zahavi's study strongly suggests that welfare capitalism, not simply adversarial relations between management and labor, has long been an important thread in the story of industrial relations in the United States.

The company town, such as this community owned by the Wheeling Steel Corporation photographed in 1874, was an extreme example of business involvement in the community.

civic responsibilities? Did those views change with evolving market and competitive environments?

The Business Firm and Government

The relationships between the firm and the local, state, and federal governments are usually an interesting part of the environment encountered by the business firm historically. Although Americans, whether or not they are entrepreneurs, like to think of themselves as independent of the government, the fact remains that business life is inextricably bound up with the law and governmental authority. This relationship is all the more complex in the United States because the firm's executives have to deal with government at three levels, local, state, and federal, and in government's judicial, legislative, and executive capacities.

All but the simplest of business firms exist and operate under some form of government charter. This charter will probably have provided a starting point in the investigation of the nearby firm. (The charter is sometimes one of the few documents retained by a firm from its early history.) Thus essential questions for the historian include: What legal form has the firm taken? From whom has the business received its charter? Has this legal situation changed over time? If so, how?

Aside from the chartering of the firm, governments in the United States have related to business with policies of development and of regulation. Generally, developmental policies began before regulatory policies, but the two also existed side by side. Regulatory policies that restrict a business executive's freedom to act from purely private considerations have usually generated the most controversy in government-business relations, and those of us exploring the history of a firm expect to find some evidence of controversy. But do not be misled into overlooking less controversial elements of the governmental environment for the conduct of business in the United States.

There was a long tradition in American government, going back into colonial times, of providing assistance for the development of entrepreneurial activity. Was the firm under exploration part of that tradition? This developmental assistance was often indirect. Developmental assistance from government often has shaped the history of entire industries, no less than the firms that comprise them. For the person exploring the history of an intercity trucking firm, for instance, the construction of the interstate highway network after 1956 would have a major influence on shaping the history of that firm. Developmental assistance often occurred with transportation projects. In American history, governments at all levels have been active in developing roads, highways, airports, waterways, and railroads for private firms to use.

Direct government assistance may also have shaped the course of a firm's history. At the federal level, for example, companies have lobbied historically for tariff protection from foreign competition. If the firm under study is one in which there was a potential for foreign competition, then it is necessary to ask about the possibilities of tariff protection shaping the history of the organization. Since 1933 agricultural firms have received direct subsidies from the federal government through the U.S. Department of Agriculture. Direct government assistance has been common at the state and local levels as well. Local and state tax abatements, loans, and the like, for developmental purposes, were part of the American business environment in the twentieth century from which the firm under study may have benefited. Just as the student of the nearby business wants to remain sensitive to the sorts of indirect assistance government provided the firm, so too will he or she remain aware of the possibilities of the firm having received some form of direct governmental aid.

If both direct and indirect developmental assistance from one or more levels of government may have provided an environment that shaped the history of the firm, regulation may have affected the company profoundly. Local governments regulated business entrepreneurs' activities as early as the first colonial years. The federal government did not become powerfully involved with the regulation of business, however, until the first decade of the twentieth century. Some state governments began to regulate businesses before 1900. But the subject of regulation will most likely concern the exploration of the nearby history of the twentieth century. Although the nineteenth century was never a time of laissez faire in the American political economy, public intrusion into the affairs of business was usually for the purpose of developing opportunities, not checking unbridled private power.

Government regulation of business during the twentieth century has involved reducing the independence of the business executive. Twentieth-century entrepreneurs have to take into account a more complex society than did their nineteenth-century counterparts. The fact that regulation has confronted business executives with human factors arising from political forces outside of their direct control has caused a large volume of complaint from men and women in business regarding their reduced freedoms. But in dealing with the subject of regulation, historians are cognizant that business leaders have as often as not welcomed regulation in the past.

Government regulation of business was not necessarily hostile toward entrepreneurship or business interests. As we have already seen, business leaders historically tried to control the uncertainties of price competition. In the twentieth century government regulation provided them with new opportunities for making the conduct of business less uncertain. Predictability was an important attribute for investors, especially as the sums involved became huge. Thus the historian of the firm must realize that the business leaders under study may have welcomed government regulation, and may have worked to achieve regulation in the first instance. The federal government created the Interstate Commerce Commission in 1887 and began its first hesitant steps toward regulation, for instance. Some railroad executives had advocated the new policy because they expected federal regulation to help them administer prices based on their analyses of costs, regardless of competition between lines. The notion that business was invariably against regulation remains one of the least well-founded myths of American history. The student exploring the history of a firm must avoid preconceptions of the subject.

But if business opposition to regulation was a myth, truthful experiences underlie it, as is usually the case with myths. Business involvement in support of or in opposition to regulation depended on the case at hand, the situation of the moment, and the industry under study. Although the federal antitrust statutes that began with the Sherman Act of 1890 failed to prevent the concentration of assets into fewer and fewer firms, antitrust policies have sometimes had the effect of guarding the interests of smaller firms facing competition from larger, wealthier, and more powerful competitors. Regulatory policies forbid large chain stores, for instance, from deliberately losing money in one market for a time in order to wrest a market share from smaller, locally based stores. Executives of the large chain learned to live with the regulations while proprietors of smaller stores called upon elected officials to maintain the regulations. Yet both might have united at some time in a common political effort to overthrow government regulations that, for instance, required them to bargain with their employees' trade unions.

The history of government regulation is obviously a subject that is far too complex to discuss fully here. Government regulation of business has increased as the twentieth century has unfolded. Since 1960, when environmental concerns began to intrude on public consciousness and the environmental movement was born, businesses have had to deal with complex regulations concerning the natural environment and, for lack of a better term, the quality of life. Firms have responded to those new kinds of regulations differently, depending on the personalities of their leaders, the competitive situation being faced, and the nature of the industry. There are no special problems facing the business historian regarding regulation that all historians do not face when they ask questions imaginatively and sift through evidence.

Suggested Readings

Alfred D. Chandler, Jr., "The Beginnings of 'Big Business' in American Industry," reprinted in *Managing Big Business: Essays from the Business History Review* (Richard S. Tedlow and Richard R. John, Jr., eds.; Boston: Harvard Business School Press, 1986), 2-32, originally published in 1959, is the classic statement about the importance of the market for the rise of big business. See also Chandler's "The Emergence of Managerial Capitalism," ibid., 368-397.

Changes in the steel industry may fascinate the local historian because that industry was so important a part of the industrial society built after the Civil War. Harold Livesay, *Andrew Carnegie and the Rise of Big Business* (Boston: Little, Brown, 1975) is a brief account.

The standard biography is Joseph Frazier Wall, *Andrew Carnegie* (New York: Oxford University Press, 1970). Historians have told the story of recent changes in the steel industry. See John P. Hoerr, *And The Wolf Finally Came: The Decline of the American Steel Industry* (Pittsburgh: University of Pittsburgh Press, 1988) and Paul A. Tiffany, *The Decline of American Steel* (New York: Oxford University Press, 1988).

Mary Yeager's study of the meat-packing industry during the late nineteenth and early twentieth centuries, *Competition and Regulation: The Development of Oligopoly in the Meat Industry* (Greenwich, CT: JAI Press, 1981), is the standard account. The historian of today's meat packer will find the industry organized very differently than it was as recently as the middle of the twentieth century. Firms have left Chicago for packing sites in the Great Plains. Ralph L. Nelson, *Merger Movements in American Industry, 1895-1956* (Princeton: Princeton University Press, 1959) is the classic statement. A recent analysis of the first merger wave is Naomi R. Lamoreaux, *The Great Merger Movement in American Business, 1895-1904* (New York: Cambridge University Press, 1985).

Roland Marchand, *Advertising the American Dream: Making Way for Modernity, 1920-1940* (Berkeley and Los Angeles: University of California Press, 1985) stands as a history of advertising solidly based on a review of both advertisements themselves and the archives of advertising agencies. The seminal works on the history of marketing are Susan Strasser, *Satisfaction Guaranteed: The Making of The American Mass Market* (New York: Pantheon Books, 1989) and Richard Tedlow, *New and Improved: The Story of Mass Marketing in America* (New York: Basic Books, 1990).

·4·

Local Business History—Internal Sources

FINDING SOURCES OF HISTORICAL INFORMATION WITHIN the business firm provides exciting opportunities and interesting challenges. In the records left by succeeding generations of owners, partners, directors, managers, engineers, accountants, and promoters (prime examples of those first-hand historical records that historians call sources), can be found the threads with which to weave a historical account. This chapter suggests how to gather the warp and woof from which to create an interesting and useful fabric. A historical investigator soon discovers that much more is involved than pouring over dusty records and faded photographs, however much delight can be experienced in discovering and exploring those remains of the past. Explorations and discoveries become all the more rewarding not just as new answers are discovered, but as they spark interest in new questions as well.

A rigorous research approach to a firm's records begins with the most general records and proceeds to the more specific and specialized material that will enlarge meaning and significance. This book uses the convention among historians of distinguishing between *primary* and *secondary* sources. *Primary sources* include internal business records generated by participants at the time of events. *Secondary sources* include works about those events, usually generated at some distance in time and by someone other than the participants. (A memoir by a participant blurs the distinction between primary and secondary records.) Of course, internal business records, or primary sources about the firm, always need to be studied in light of appropriate secondary sources. Beginning an exploration of the firm's internal records with some understanding of the larger picture allows a historian

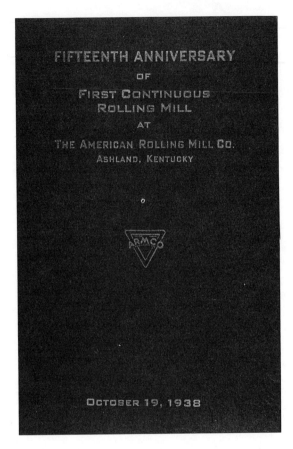

FIFTEENTH ANNIVERSARY

OF

FIRST CONTINUOUS
ROLLING MILL

AT

THE AMERICAN ROLLING MILL CO.
ASHLAND, KENTUCKY

ARMCO

OCTOBER 19, 1938

Anniversaries often provide the impetus for retrospective examinations of the firm's accomplishments. Identifying important anniversaries and concentrating on company publications around that date often allow the historian quick access to important data.

to ask the most fruitful questions of the sources. Thus it is generally best to work from the most general to the more specific sources, always with questions that focus attention, a keen eye for change, and a willingness to relate findings to what others have observed. Sources are in the end like any other tools—no matter what the quality, their value, in large part, lies with the skill of the user.

This chapter gives attention to the types of records that the historian is most likely to encounter in nearby business history research. But it is important to understand at the outset that anything like a comprehensive listing of all of the possible internal sources is impossible in a small book.

Businesses of different types have produced very different kinds of records. Since the American environment has fostered diversity, the best that this book can do is to mention the broad categories. And of course much will depend on what the firm has saved. As mentioned in the first chapter, some firms maintain professionally run archives, but they are the exception. More likely research will entail searching for and digging through old files in remote recesses of a firm's offices.

Questions to Ask About a Firm

Chapter 2 examined the questions to be considered before approaching a firm's records. These questions are critical to understanding the sources available regarding the founding, growth, and development of a business. Without questions to serve as a guide, the historian is adrift in a featureless sea of facts and figures. Expressed differently, the questions one asks of the sources will direct the inquiry. Questions will guide the historian to sources and, even within the context of a given source, will focus attention on selected information.

One word of caution at the outset: no one can formulate all the important questions before he or she commences the actual research. Inevitably, new questions appear as the examination of the historical sources continues. Frequently, these *secondary* questions will call attention to conditions that have set the particular business apart from others in the industry or the geographic area.

Raising these *secondary* questions will enrich an investigation as research proceeds, for they will lead to a comprehension of the dynamics of change within the firm. For example, a manufacturing company might be seen to have achieved increased production; that observation should lead to an important set of *secondary* questions. Was there a technical innovation used? Who favored it? Who was opposed to it? If there was opposition, what were the firm's internal processes of reaching decisions that overcame the resistance to innovation? Answers to such *secondary* questions—and they are secondary only because they followed a first question that led to the discovery of increased production—provide insights into the decision-making process, the personalities, and the tensions that drove the business. Searching for answers to such questions results in a richer account of the firm's history. Questions that arise as research progresses may well force a return to documents previously covered or a search for new insights from old data. In the process, the historian acquires an intimate knowledge of a subject that allows not only a mastery of the facts, but also an understanding of the spirit and character that define the organization. Such intimacy is gratifying, producing an interpretation that is much more compelling than the sum of the facts.

Background Information: Obtaining an Overview

The pursuit of history ideally begins with the general and proceeds to the specific, taking into account what previous researchers have found. Exploring the history of a local business usually involves evaluating the subject comparatively. Practically speaking this comparison means beginning research by attempting to obtain an overview of the industry of which a particular firm is a part. Many industries have histories that can serve as a starting point. Some bibliographic resources to help locate histories of particular industries have already been suggested. If several histories are available, it is wisest to select the most recent and work back to the oldest.

There are several possible locations of the sort of general history where the student of a local firm might find useful background material. Industrial histories are not always books. Trade journals sometime contain articles on the history of the industry or the leading firms in the industry. While these pieces may appear at any point in time, significant anniversaries or the passing of key individuals often provide the impetus for a valuable retrospective article in a trade magazine or paper.

Secondary works, even if they are sketchy or do not focus on the firm under study, provide local business historians with an important starting point. While reading the secondary works, a useful technique is to develop an outline that includes dates of key events, the changes that have affected the industry and individual firms, and the personalities recognized as important. In addition to gathering information about the industry, it is useful to look for information about the firm, other firms in the locality, and individuals associated with the firm under study who made important contributions. Such recognition provides the first clue to important facets of the firm's development. If the studies contain citations to sources or if the author has included a bibliography, close attention should be paid to these sources. Reading narratives at the outset of an exploration of a local business's history may save time later in the research process by identifying valuable primary resources.

As well as reviewing the history of the industry, the historian doing research in the records of a local business takes time to become familiar with the history of a firm's locality. Almost every county and town has a local history that outlines important events, identifies the more significant personalities, and describes institutions in the area. Local conditions, some of which may not be apparent, often have played a role in the establishment and development of business. For example, the discovery of natural gas in northwestern Ohio was responsible for several glass manufacturing companies locating in that area. The state prison in Columbus, Ohio, a source of cheap labor, was a major factor in the decision to organize tool companies in the state capital. Changes in business may also have been influenced by local conditions. The construction of a railroad, for example, may have exposed a firm to more intense competition while it opened new markets. Conversely, internal changes in a firm may have an impact on the community that altered its business environment. Responses to labor problems frequently have had far-reaching consequences for the relations between a business and its community, for example.

Armed with a general understanding of the industry and a knowledge of its local environment, the historian can turn to the firm's internal history. Here again it is best to begin with a study of the general sources and then proceed to the more specific. Businesses more than a generation old often will have a printed history. This history may have been published in pamphlet or book form, or it may have appeared in newsletters. Shorter historical treatments found in employee newsletters or in advertising materials may not be as well known and hence may be more difficult to find. Although these histories can appear at any point in a company's development, anniversaries frequently prompted an interest that led to the writing of historical accounts.

Business historians surveying a firm's records are often pleasantly surprised to find either manuscript histories or clippings from printed sources tucked away in file cabinets or desk drawers somewhere in the firm's offices. Sometimes these materials are unpublished histories written by an employee, retired employee, or owner. For example, *Our Sun*, the employee magazine for the Sun Oil Corporation, published historical articles. In 1956 *Our Sun* published six articles that examined the history of innovations and individuals in the firm who had contributed to the industry in some important way. Local publications are another source for company histories. If the firm is important to the local economy, if it has celebrated a

Shop Talk

Riesbeck's

• WOODSFIELD   • BARNESVILLE
• ST. CLAIRSVILLE • ELM GROVE   • CAMBRIDGE

RIESBECK'S EMPLOYEE PUBLICATION JEAN THOMPSON EDITOR **MARCH 1987**

IT WAS ALL STARTED BY A WIDOW WITH FIVE CHILDREN

MARGARET M. RIESBECK [1886-1970] FOUNDER

After becoming a widow with five small children in 1921, Margaret Riesbeck opened a small dry goods and grocery store in Woodsfield, Ohio. They relocated to Martins Ferry in 1933, with the help of her children, operated three neighborhood type grocery stores. Two of her sons, Charles P. and Bernard are deceased. Her surviving daughters, Mary Theurich and Marguerite Pocsik live in Martins Ferry, and Paul M. Riesbeck, Sr. resides in St. Clairsville. She would be proud of her decendants who have helped to carry on the family business:

GRANDCHILDREN: Richard L. Riesbeck, William B. Riesbeck, Bernard Riesbeck - Martins Ferry Office; Paul M. Riesbeck, Jr. - Elm Grove #5; J.D. Riesbeck, Anthony Alan Riesbeck - St. Clairsville #8. GREAT GRANDCHILDREN: Kimberly Riesbeck, Judy Sulek, Jackie Donathan - St. Clairsville #8; Charles M. Riesbeck - Cambridge #4.

To insure another 66 years of our company, it will take dedication and hard work from all of us at Riesbeck Food Markets, Inc.

Company newsletters often contain articles that recount important events in the company's history. In this issue of *Shop Talk*, an employee newsletter published by Riesbeck's Stores of Wheeling, West Virginia, the editor has included a biography of the founder and the second generation of family managers.

significant anniversary or undergone important changes (such as a merger or bankruptcy) there is a good chance that it has been featured in the local press, chamber of commerce literature, or regional publications. While working on a history of the Wheeling Pittsburgh Steel Corporation several years ago, for example, one of us found that several of the firms that combined to form this company in the early 1920s were featured in a series of articles published in the *Wheeling Intelligencer,* the local newspaper. Similar discoveries were made for several glass and pottery companies in the Ohio Valley. Firms that existed during the late nineteenth and early twentieth centuries were often featured in county histories or regional historical atlases. Authors of these publications typically sold space to business or professional men and women who wrote brief descriptions of their firms. Such sources provide particularly useful information—often otherwise unavailable data—on law firms, merchandising houses, and transportation enterprises. Also, local histories and atlases are often good sources for images of a firm's facilities, leaders, and employees. More recently, almost every city has a popular history that contains information on its major businesses, often stories that approach our own time.

The firm itself is likely to have some sort of history in its files, or at least a file of materials about it of the sort described. One of us found manuscripts dealing with the history of Union Fork and Hoe, a tool company in Columbus, Ohio, in the firm's files. None were complete, but taken together, those manuscript histories provided a good starting point from which to approach the company's records. In the end, two of the manuscripts proved particularly valuable because they contained marginal notes that offered an unusual opportunity to understand how corporate officers at various points in the firm's development viewed the business. Even when a firm has a published history, review of the manuscript drafts may offer insights, and stimulate questions that are especially valuable when launching a project.

The absence of published or manuscript materials in a company's files is not necessarily an indication that such sources do not exist. Occasionally they can be found at local libraries or historical societies. Since the fate of every community has been linked to its economic enterprises, local historians and librarians have sometimes preserved annual reports, advertising literature, photographs, and the papers of prominent businessmen and businesswomen. These sources might even prove more complete for earlier periods than the firm's own internal records. Finally, local or regional historical society publications should be consulted. These societies often publish articles that contain information about business and industries in the region they serve. A recent survey of the periodical literature of the Ohio Historical Society, for example, revealed information on the Hocking Valley Railroad, the Leffel Turbine Company, and the Plymouth Motor Car Company. These publications may also contain reviews of published works and check lists of unpublished dissertations and theses that will prove useful.

Once the local historian has located sources that will provide an overview of the firm, has identified the key individuals, and has pointed to events that previous authors have felt to be important, the task at hand is cautious, critical reading. It is wise to be wary of the possible shortcomings of secondary sources. First, histories written for or published by the firm usually interpret the past from management's perspective. These works focus on the accomplishments of a few individuals who are portrayed favorably. More desirable history reflects critical thought that places individuals in context, accurately evaluating the individual's contributions and identifying the impersonal forces that shaped the firm. Second, the histories of well-established firms often focus on the founders and the management corps in power at the time the history was written. Businesses survive by constant adjustment to a changing environment. Hence, every generation of leaders is faced with important decisions that, to a greater or lesser extent, shape the firm. The critical business historian becomes aware of the roles of different groups of people within the firm. Third, most internally produced histories tend to concentrate on the firm's successes. This focus unfolds despite the fact that an analysis can produce a better understanding of how (and why) a firm developed in a particular way if it includes failures along with successes. Fourth, corporate histories often ignore the impact of forces outside the firm. Chapter 3 explained several basic forces that shaped businesses, including the development of markets, changing business structures, and government regulation. A critical business historian is aware that internal histories, or accounts prepared for public relations purposes, although valuable sources of information, often overlooked or grossly misinterpreted external factors. Fifth, many histories are incomplete. They do not bring the business up-to-date; they superficially treat aspects of the business for which the internal record is sketchy; or they overlook innovations in business techniques. The last shortcoming almost always is present in the older firm histories. Sixth, internal histories tend to ignore the significance of the commonplace. For example, in the histories of the Wheeling Pittsburgh Steel Corporation, the writers completely ignored accounting innovations that had been made in the decade after the Civil War. When the histories were prepared in the 1920s, industrial cost accounting was taken for granted; but in the 1860s, when Wheeling Pittsburgh Steel executives pioneered in their use of industrial cost accounting, it was a powerful, exciting new tool that allowed management to monitor operations and to make decisions about the potential impact of new technology.

The shortcomings, however, need not be a burden. All of these shortcomings can be identified and can become the basis for secondary questions if sources are approached critically, if background research on the industry has been done, and if the secondary literature on business history has become familiar. Correcting the mistakes of previous writers is an obligation that one assumes when he or she undertakes the preparation of a history. In doing so, historians can provide their audiences with a fresh perspective that is important if the past is to be relevant to the present.

The Sources

Once permission has been obtained to enter a company's archives, the historian needs to consider the types of records that may be found there. It is unlikely that all of potentially available types of records will exist for any one firm. The value of those that are available will depend on what questions need to be answered and on the diligence with which the firm has maintained its records. While the questions the historian brings to these sources will determine the relative significance of each one, some general principles apply to their use. First, one must always be alert for changes and be prepared to explain why such changes have occurred. If, for example, in reading the minutes of the board of directors the researcher discovers the creation of a new committee structure, it is appropriate to seek an explanation. Second, it is important to avoid becoming so immersed in a particular series of records as to lose sight of how they relate to the larger picture. For example, when examining the records of a board of directors, the historian exploring a local business needs to keep in mind what was occurring in the industry and what were the general economic conditions—the context, in other words, in which the board members deliberated the firm's policies. Third, it is well to realize the likely need to supplement information from one source with that from another in order to achieve full understanding. For example, biographical research on individual members of the board of directors might help the historian to understand the relationships that undergirded the functioning of the group. Likewise, it may be necessary to do background reading on technical processes, local geography, or even the relative value of money to understand accurately a primary source. Fourth, the historian must be sensitive to omissions such as the unnoted departure of important individuals, or the lack of notice of economic events. In other words, the absence of information may provide clues to what the managers saw as important.

A major reason that relatively few historians have studied the development of small businesses in America has been the failure to preserve the records of small businesses, especially those that go out of existence. One of the few industries dominated by small businesses to receive the attention of historians has been the cutlery industry of the Connecticut Valley. In her *A History of the Cutlery Industry in the Connecticut Valley* (Northampton, Mass.: Smith College Studies in History, 1955), Martha Taber presents an account of the development of the leading firms in the cutlery industry from their establishment in the 1830s through World War II. Unlike the case in many industries composed of small businesses, in the cutlery industry many of the same firms had been in existence for decades. Taber was fortunate in having a wide range of corporate records, but especially the minutes of the meetings of boards of directors, upon which to draw. Records of the Russell Company and the Ames Company, made available to Taber through personal connections with people associated with those two firms, proved especially valuable. From these records she was able to determine corporate growth strategies, management structures, and technological innovations, along with the nature of interactions between the companies, especially their involvement in trade associations, and the nature of their labor relations.

Board Records

The broadest perspective of the firm's development will be found in the minutes of the governing body, such as the board of directors or managing partners. Under the best of circumstances the minutes and related documents will record actions taken by this body or board and summarize the deliberations that led to these actions. Depending on the skill of the secretary and the needs of the business, these minutes may also contain other helpful information.

A good way to begin exploring the board minutes is to examine the members. Compiling a short biography of each board member may be useful, as already noted. It is wise to look for ties that may shed light on how individual members related to each other. Although the types of relationships will differ from firm to firm and even from time to time within a firm, and from city to city, business historians generally explore several characteristics of personal relationships among the men and women at the highest level of responsibility for the firm. First, family relationships are important to sketch. Since many businesses began as family enterprises it is important to examine the connections between the role of the family as an institution and the firm's leadership, and the impact of kinship relationships on business decisions. Even where the firm is not a *family business* one should be aware of family ties in management, and skilled job areas. Second, long term business and social relationships apart from the family are meaningful to chart. Did the firm's leaders share memberships in other institutions, such as fraternities, sororities, country clubs, or churches? Did they serve together in other contexts, such as in service clubs? Were there old school ties in which board members had educational experiences in common? Did leaders share professional backgrounds, say as attorneys, engineers, or accountants? Did they come from the same neighborhood? Such questions allow the local historian to develop an accurate picture of the personal and social relationships of the firm's topmost leadership, whether board members or partners.

After giving thought to this first level of personal characteristics and social relationships of the board members, as a rule historians want to consider a second level of information of how a firm's officers related to their industry and to their local business community. This information will allow an evaluation of how the firm interacted with its competition, its customers, and its suppliers. Again, there are several questions to ask. Were there board members who held offices in trade associations, regulatory agencies, or support industries? Did board members serve on the boards of other businesses? For example, discovering that board members of a manufacturing firm also served on the board of a bank, or vice versa, typically leads to important questions of how the firm raised capital, and how it might have been subject to control from outside. Were there board members who had family or other relationships with competitive firms? One of us discovered that a father-son combination held board positions in the two largest manufacturers of hand tools. Knowing this relationship allowed closer scrutiny of competitive practices in the industry and helped explain how executives transferred information from firm to firm.

The historian has available many sources of biographical, family, and career information on the people who hold important positions within business organizations. In the next chapter, we will suggest a systematic approach to finding information outside of the firm itself. Within the firm, or very close to it, the local historian may encounter local histories, obituary notices, and biographical dictionaries, that reveal family or social relationships. Private collections of correspondence may help in understanding the personal, social, business, and community relationships of a firm's top officers. The records of other businesses may even be worth exploring in this regard. The extra effort to uncover information, which on the surface may seem to lead away from the central purpose of writing a firm's history, may provide a depth of insight that otherwise would escape attention.

The composition of the board is another important area to observe. Board organization is often indicative of the firm's entire structure. Business historians studying a board of directors look for committees, note their functions, and see who the key members were. They examine how the committees interacted with staff members, with other committees, and the full board. They observe whether or not board members were involved with the daily affairs of the firm. Understanding board organization and how it changed helps the historian explain how the firm's leadership arrived at decisions. If the board gave more attention to one aspect of the company's operations, the researcher gains insight into what the board thought to be important at any given point in the firm's development, and what criteria the leaders used to define the success or failure of operations. Careful attention to the sources of information that the board used in its decision making provides important clues. In a larger, more complex firm, the control of the flow of information sometimes allowed professional management to wield considerable power.

Clearly it is worthwhile to explore how the board defined its relationship with management. Students of business usually distinguish between *inside* and *outside* appointments to a firm's board of directors, the *inside* members being those managers appointed to the board, and the *outside* members those persons on the board who have no other direct relationship to the firm. This awareness is useful for understanding who controls the company, the management, or other parties. Who was directly responsible to the board? How were decisions communicated/implemented? It is particularly important to analyze changes in the types of decisions the board viewed as its prerogative, and in the types of information that it used. Changes in these areas may be signals that the board was reacting to problems, that it was reassessing its role, that changes were occurring in management techniques. Such changes may best be explained by relating them to what was learned about the industry, the environment in which the firm operated.

There are two important general sources of information about a board of directors aside from the minutes of meetings and other related material filed with those minutes. What might be called the *official* records of the firm are likely to be very important. Reports to stockholders allow examination of how the board presented the operation of the firm to one very important group, the owners. The minutes of stockholder meetings also will prove useful. Information found in the annual reports to the stockholders contrasting with the content of board meeting minutes can provide insight into the firm's most conspicuous successes and failures. As chapter 5 will explain, in addition to reports to the stockholders, businesses have also filed reports with governmental units that define segments of its operations. If those reporting requirements can be identified and copies of reports obtained, either from the company files or from the agency, a mine of data often can be found.

The private correspondence of individuals, or logs of telephone calls, are documents that historians prize. In some instances an individual's letters may be in the firm's files, while in other cases they may be in the collection of a library or historical society, or in the possession of the family. Particularly for key board members and important managers, correspondence should be consulted. For instance, letters from S. P. Bush, president of Buckeye Steel, to his wife provided one of us with a fresh perspective and consequently shed light on motivation.

Management Records

For an understanding of a firm's operations, business historians seek to examine several types of information. The types of management records available will depend, of course, upon a number of factors. These factors include the sort of business in which the firm was engaged and how long it conducted that business. Another factor, of course, is historical accident: just what has survived in a firm's files is often a matter of chance. A warehouse filled with paper, or only a few ledgers and an occasional file cabinet may comprise the company archives. These records may be well organized or filed in confusion. They may be fairly complete or highly selective. Whatever the state of the firm's records it is critically important to approach the records with a well thought out plan based on the questions raised.

Since every business is the producer of a good or service, a logical point to begin is with the records that shed light on the firm's product. A study

Accounting records, such as this trial balance sheet, show expenses and income. While such documents may be a valuable source of specific information, examination over a period of time may allow for the most important insights. Comparisons often make trends apparent or point out sharp changes in costs, sources of supply, or income.

of the range of the firm's products and services, and a review of the patterns of output, paying close attention to changes in production patterns, is enlightening. The business historian needs to be particularly sensitive to dramatic increases or decreases in the firm's output and be prepared to examine internal, as well as external, forces that may be responsible. In arriving at explanations, an awareness of what was happening in the industry, and more generally in the economy, makes it possible to relate the activities of a firm to the broader picture and to discern the relative importance of internal and external factors.

When the individual firm, or perhaps a group of firms within an industry, experienced a performance pattern radically different from the industry as a whole or from the nation's general economic cycle of prosperity and depression, it is essential to scrutinize the records for indications of internal factors that set the firm apart. For example, during the decade after the Civil War, a few nail manufacturers in the upper Ohio Valley prospered while others faltered. All were selling in the same market, all were marketing their product at the same price, yet some were showing large profits while others were losing money. This pattern suggested that internal factors varied and directed attention to a more intensive study of technology, cost management, sales techniques, and raw materials procurement.

Once the patterns of performance are clear, explaining them may require further background reading. Experienced scholars have learned that an understanding of primary sources often requires combining an inquiry into the firm's internal records with parallel research in the secondary literature. (Suggestions for locating secondary literature in business history will be found at the end of each chapter.) A familiarity with the stage of development of technology or business techniques at a given time is usually essential in determining whether or not a firm was advanced or obsolete. Again, the history of the cut nail industry illustrates the point. In order to determine whether or not the favorable performance noted above was a result of differentials among firms in their technologies, the researcher had to examine the technology available to the industry. After a survey of the secondary literature, it soon became apparent that a technological breakthrough was not responsible for the difference in performance. The profitable firms in question were using the same machines and processes as their less successful competitors. Once technology was ruled out, the research turned to sales and management policies. Again, nothing suggested that the successful manufacturers were using unique sales techniques. In the case of management techniques however, a major discrepancy appeared. The successful firms had introduced an elementary form of cost accounting that allowed management to make decisions about material purchases and to link stages in the production process effectively. This observation provided the key that allowed a thorough examination of management techniques and eventually a clearer understanding of how the firm's executives arrived at planning, marketing, and technological decisions.

After gaining a good comprehension of the firm's production patterns, it may be desirable to turn to the records of the various departments or units that make up the firm. Here, the process is essentially the same. It is useful to gain an overview of the activities of departments or areas that seem to be most significant to the firm's development as well as to look for changes, the appearance of problems, and at how units relate to one another within the firm.

Legal Records

Legal records are often useful sources of information about a company's activities. Legal records may be located in the company archives or may be scattered throughout the various departments of the company. Or they may be found in the files of law firms retained by the company. We have found legal records to be especially useful in revealing connections between companies. Contracts show various forms of company interactions. Contracts may, for instance, show how companies cooperated in the development of natural resources and markets. A 1907 contract between the Federal Glass Company and the Buckeye Steel Castings Company, both of Columbus, Ohio, showed how the two firms agreed to prospect jointly for a new source of energy, natural gas. Or legal records may reveal conflict between companies. Buckeye Steel's legal records showed clearly how the corporation sought to avoid unfriendly takeovers by other companies in the 1970s.

Accounting Records

Every firm maintains some sort of financial records to describe its activities. The history of a local business is incomplete unless financial records are located and examined. Financial records may be simple ledger books or they may be very complex. The accounting records were important raw data from which owners and managers made a range of decisions. To exploit the firm's financial records fully in reconstructing its history, it is best to begin the study of accounting data at the highest level, looking first at reports made to the board and then work back through lower levels in the organization.

Accounting records are likely to be a very revealing source for a business history. In the least complex firms the records will provide data on who was purchasing the firm's products or services, how much they cost, where the firm acquired supplies, and the differential between costs and income. In some instances, these records will also allow an estimation of how much the firm was producing, where the firm was selling products or services, and the major cost categories. More complex financial records provide precise descriptions of the internal operations. They break the cost per unit down into components such as labor, materials, overhead, and mathematically relate the various inputs. For example, such records may state the number of nails per ton of metal, or the number of rakes per man hour of time. Those ratios were important bits of information since they furnished management with insights that allowed an objective evaluation of efficiency.

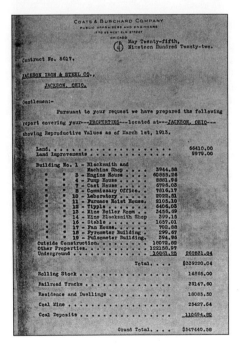

Auditors' reports, such as this one from the files of the Jackson Iron and Steel Company, provide the historian with an overview of the company's assets. Close examination of such records can reveal much about the firm. For example, this document describes a firm that is integrated (it owned mines, factories, and transportation facilities) and owned considerable amounts of undeveloped real estate and housing.

In his history of a small business, *Small Business in Brass Manufacturing: The Smith & Griggs Co. of Waterbury* (New York: New York University Press, 1956), Theodore Marburg made excellent use of corporate records—minutes of board of directors' meetings, correspondence to and from executives, and accounting reports—available in the Yale University library to reconstruct the evolution of the company. The development of specialty products and, thus, a market niche, management by hard-driving entrepreneurs eager to adopt new production technologies, and the maintenance of close, friendly, personal relationships with wholesalers buying its products brought growth and prosperity to Smith & Griggs between its founding in 1865 and about 1908. Conversely, the erosion of all of those factors after 1908, when a new president assumed office, led to the decline of the company. Letters coming into Smith & Griggs after 1910 showed, for instance, that the company's customers were increasingly unhappy with the quality of the service provided them, and accounting records revealed that the company spent few funds on improvements in how its products were made. Saddled with a management unable to solve its problems, Smith & Griggs went out of existence in 1936.

Marketing and Advertising

In our experience, marketing records were essential for understanding a critically significant part of a firm's history: what was its market, what was its strategy for reaching that market, and how successfully did it achieve its goals? Marketing records provide a description of how the firm distributed goods or services, where it sold products, who was purchasing the firm's goods and services, and usually some indication of the company's gross income. For businesses that produced raw materials or semifinished products, marketing may have been a relatively simple activity of sales to a few other firms, while the producer of consumer goods may have sold to a very wide and complex market indeed. In every case, the firm had a stated or implied market strategy that defined the type of customer that it sought to reach. It is therefore necessary to understand this strategy in order to evaluate how effective the company was in realizing its goals.

Beginning in the late nineteenth century and continuing into the twentieth century, evaluation of existing and potential markets became an

Product catalogs provide important information about the firm's marketing strategy. The Geo. L. Mesker & Co. catalog, shown here, not only described the product but contained letters from customers and a listing, by state, of the addresses of customers.

increasingly important activity for many firms. The wise business historian pays close attention to how the firm's executives defined their market, what tools they used in that process, and what changes occurred in both the market and the tools used to understand it. For the historian, comprehending the market is often a key to the analysis of internal decisions that affected the growth and development of the firm. For example, Union Fork and Hoe, a hand tool manufacturer in Columbus, Ohio, concentrated on the production of shovels, rakes, and hoes for the rural market until the late 1920s. Using census figures that showed a decline in the farm population and feedback from hardware dealers who pointed to an upsurge in urban gardening, Union Fork and Hoe decided to exploit this new market by manufacturing a line of lighter tools and accompanying in-store displays with *how to* gardening pamphlets. This redefinition of its market was critical to Union Fork and Hoe's success during the next two decades.

Advertising literature is usually an integral part of a firm's marketing records. Examples of the firm's advertisements, ordinarily easy to find, can provide a rich resource for comprehending the firm's history, especially if they are examined systematically. Looking at the firm's advertisements over time, for instance, can reveal changes in advertising strategies. Changes in advertisements, and the changing strategy that they suggest, may indicate that an effort was being made to move into a new market, to gain a larger share of the existing market, or to increase unit consumption among existing customers.

Employee Relations Records

The business firm under study was a social unit as well as an economic entity, a group of people working together, interacting, and engaging in a common endeavor. The firm may have been a happy community or one characterized by social tensions. In any case, employee relations comprise an important aspect of business history. Of course, the firm's relationships with its employees will probably have much to do with its success as an economic being. The type of employees, management's attention to working conditions, training, fringe benefits, and compensation are pertinent subjects for the historian of a business firm. Just as every firm had some explicit or implicit marketing strategy, so it had an employment policy that defined the relationship between the firm and its workers. The evolving nature of those relationships will have affected the firm's production of goods and provision of services.

A starting point for the analysis of a firm's employee policy is to examine management itself. Information about key managers is usually easy to find. First, one should consider the source of management. Did family relationship play a role in selection? Did the firm promote from within? If so, was there a common pattern in those promotions (did top management come from a certain department, or from a single skill group, such as engineers or lawyers)? Or did the company seek talent from the outside? Once the recruitment and promotion patterns for management have been described, one ought to look for records that shed light on skilled and unskilled employment patterns. Did the company seek out people with a particular set of characteristics? For example, was there a high incidence of nepotism in the employee work force? What sorts of education and/or experience guidelines seem to have been important? Definition of the relationship between the firm and the employee is another important matter to consider. Did the firm take responsibility for training, or did it seek out people already trained? Was the training for skilled areas left to a worker controlled apprenticeship system or did the firm determine what constituted training and who was to be trained? More generally, did the employer extend his responsibility beyond work-related matters? Were recreational facilities and other social needs considered? Finally, what was the firm's attitude towards unions? Did this attitude change? If so, what prompted the change? Information about the employer–employee relationship can be gleaned from several sources. Some of the best are employee and union newsletters, union contracts, the contents of suggestion boxes, and recruiting literature.

Many business histories fail because the author never goes beyond the concerns of management or the culture of the central office. It is most important, particularly when examining the history of large firms, to understand the types of jobs employees performed, as well as employee policies.

Laboratory of RICHARD S. ROBERTSON, JR., E. M.

Analytical Chemist,

No. 12 Smithfield Street, nearly opposite Monongahela House.

Assays of Ores, Analyses of Minerals, Mineral and Potable Waters, Ores, Metals, Coals, and all Commercial Articles PROMPTLY made. Counsel given, and Investigations made, in all branches of Technical Chemistry.

SPECIAL ATTENTION GIVEN TO BLAST FURNACES.

Pittsburgh, June 24th 1873.

Report of Analysis of Coal marked —
"Webb Lower"
{ For Belfont Iron Works Co.,
Ironton Ohio. }

Water	6.61
Volatile Combustible matter	28.65
Fixed Carbon (or Coke)	59.49
Ash	3.62
Sulphur	1.63
	100.00

R. S. Robertson, jr.

Company archives frequently contain technical records, such as this chemist's report made for the Belfont Ironworks of Ironton, Ohio, in 1873. Such records can serve the historian in many ways. In this instance, the record proved that the managers of this iron furnace had turned to outside experts for assistance at a date much earlier than previously believed.

Research and Development Records

Depending on the nature of the firm's business, information contained in the files of product research and development departments may be important. If initial inquiries suggest that the firm's success was a result of improved production technology, or products, the process that led to this advantage should be examined. The most obvious source of such information is patent and copyright files that document such innovations. The absence of these files does not necessarily indicate the lack of innovation, however. Indeed, much improvement in manufacturing technology came from incremental improvements that were seldom patented or copyrighted. While evidence of such improvements is often difficult to find, several sources may hint that they were occurring. For example, improvements in outputs without corresponding capital expenditures may suggest that incremental innovation was a factor. The reminiscences of engineers or, in an earlier day, craftsmen, who often dwell on these small "unsung" changes is yet another possible source. Contents of suggestion boxes, and occasionally employee newsletters, may also contain useful information. In addition to examining how technological changes materialized, it is helpful to determine who guided the research, how much awareness there was of

In his *The Making of American Industrial Research: Science and Business at General Electric and Bell, 1876-1926* (New York: Cambridge University Press, 1985) Leonard Reich made extensive use of the records of the research laboratories of the companies he was studying to explore the relationships between corporate growth strategies and research activities. He found that a desire for market control stimulated much of the research work. In 1900 General Electric set up the first corporate research laboratory in America to advance the technology needed to maintain the company's hegemony over the nation's electric lighting market. Only after the laboratory successfully defended the company's markets through the development of the ductile-tungstun light filiment in 1911, was it allowed to move on to a broader range of experiments and products. Similarly, American Bell established its research laboratory to increase the company's lead over independents in telephone communications through the development of the electronic repeater.

competitive developments, and how process and product research fitted
into the firm's organization. It may be that technology only indirectly associated with the firm's product was important. For example, changes in
power sources, such as the introduction of electricity, or the installation of
telephones may have had an impact on the way it conducted business.

Product Information

In some instances the firm's products themselves provide a valuable
source of historical data. Examination of the products, for example, may
provide evidence of production and stylistic changes that had an impact on
quality. If the firm relied on incremental technological improvements, direct study of the product may be the only way to evaluate the change. An
example of this approach is David A. Hounshell's use of artifacts to reconstruct much of the history of the Singer Co. during the 1870s. Hounshell
explained his insights in *From the American System to Mass Production,
1800-1932: The Development of Manufacturing Technology in the United States*
(Baltimore: The Johns Hopkins University Press, 1984). Products may suggest or confirm shifts in attitude and emphasis within a firm. During the
1860s and 1870s, United States whiteware pottery manufacturers often cop-
ied or designed trademarks very similar to those of English competitors. In
the 1880s, as American firms improved the quality of their products, and
as agitation for a protective tariff gained momentum, distinctive marks
began to appear on American whiteware pottery. Some of those trademarks
even expressed a nationalistic defiance. Homer Laughlin, one of largest of
the Ohio Valley firms, for example, introduced a trademark that showed the
American eagle attacking the British lion.

Graphic Sources

Images, especially artists' sketches and photographs, may provide several
kinds of valuable information. Images may depict the physical facilities of
the firm in such a way as to allow evaluation of changes in the size or complexity of physical plants. In manufacturing firms, graphics will also provide
insight into processes and the types of machines used. One of us discovered
a set of eighteen photographs of the Knowls, Taylor, Knowls pottery firm of
Chester, West Virginia, showing the various departments within the plant.
The photographer had taken great pains to display the machines, the

workers, and the products that were being made at the time. The result was a source that contained much valuable information on working conditions: the distribution of jobs between men, women, and children; the technology used; and even some of the products. Although the glass negatives were undated, the contents of the images allowed their dating. There was a calendar for September, 1901, in the background of one picture, and the piece being made was a plate commemorating President William McKinley, who had been assassinated that same month.

Sketches, blueprints, and technical illustrations provide other graphic sources of particular value in understanding the technologies a firm was using. Sketches in the notes of W. F. Minchell, owner of an oil drilling and production company, provided invaluable information on the evolution of the syncline theory of petroleum accumulation, for example. This information in turn helped explain his firm's uncommon success in locating oil in the Ohio and West Virginia fields between 1865 and 1880.

Products often provide invaluable information to the historian. The "backstamp" used by the Homer Laughlin Potter of East Liverpool, Ohio, suggests that company's view of competition with English manufacturers. It shows the American eagle defeating the English lion.

In doing research on the technologies involved in the early days of the Alaskan king crab industry, Mansel Blackford was greatly aided by a movie made by Wakefield Seafoods, the company which dominated the industry in the 1940s and 1950s. Designed to be shown at trade shows for advertising purposes, the 25-minute film illustrated in detail how the crabs were caught, processed, cooked, and frozen. Since many of these techniques were no longer in use in the 1970s, when Blackford was conducting his research, and since written records on these subjects were scanty, the movie proved to be a gold mine of essential information. Interestingly, the movie was not found at corporate headquarters—by the 1970s Wakefield Seafoods had been purchased by another company and many of its records had been thrown away—but in the Seattle Public Library (Seattle was the headquarters of Wakefield Seafoods for many years).

Interviews

Frequently the business historian will find the unrecorded recollections and observations of individuals who have played a key role in the founding and development of the firm to be an important source. Arthur M. Johnson, in his study of the Sun Oil Company, *The Challenge of Change: the Sun Oil Company, 1945-1977* (Columbus: Ohio State University Press, 1983) and Mansel G. Blackford in his study of Wakefield Seafoods, *Pioneering a Modern Small Business: Wakefield Seafoods and the Alaska Frontier* (Greenwich, CT.: JAI Press, 1979), demonstrated the effectiveness of the interview for reconstructing the history of the firm.

Oral history is a well-developed research tool, and this chapter's suggested readings explain where to learn more about it. However, several important points ought to be kept in mind. Questions should be developed in advance of the interview. While there is frequently a temptation to use the interview early in the research process, the most informative interviews usually take place after study of the secondary and documentary sources has allowed formulation of precise questions and provided information with which to evaluate the subject's response.

Information gained from oral sources must be subjected to the same scrutiny as data gathered from other sources. Those new to the research process often hold the *eyewitness* in high regard. This respect should be tempered

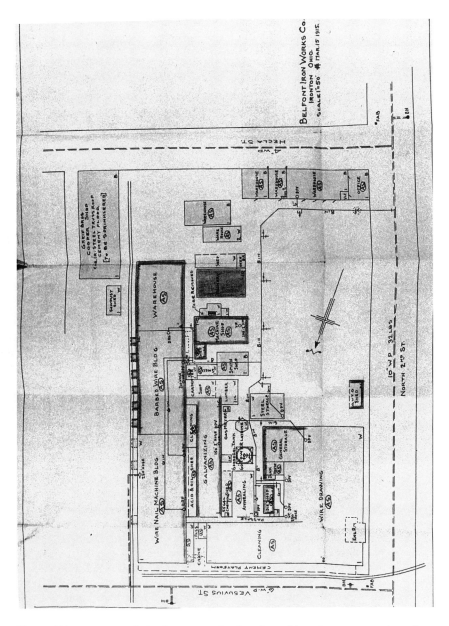

Plans and blueprints, particularly when compared with earlier and later documents, can show where expansion occurred and indicate how the manufacturing process was arranged. One of the interesting bits of information shown on this 1915 set of plans is the *auto shed* (near the center) portion of the factory. Compared with an inventory taken three years earlier that did not list this building, it pinpoints when the firm began to use gasoline-powered vehicles.

with the understanding that the eyewitness is seldom unbiased and that the passage of time inevitably blurs recollections. It is best to transcribe taped interviews. Preparing a transcription allows the subject to review his or her comments, and add to them or correct them. Generally this review improves the quality of the information. Also, transcriptions are much easier for researchers to use. Oral history interviews are among the important business history sources that should, if possible, be deposited in libraries or archives so that other students of business history can have access to them.

Conclusion

Exploring the internal records of a firm leads the historian on a fascinating journey into the past. Those internal records should help in elucidating the dynamics that propelled the business enterprise, the human uncertainty that attended decision making, and the personal satisfaction, even elation, that accompanied success. The internal records may as well help the firm's historian appreciate the crushing impact of failure. The story thus revealed may not always have high drama, but it holds much potential for expanding insightful knowledge about the individual, the family, the community, the region, and the nation. It may be disappointing to find that the firm's records on important subjects are either sketchy or missing altogether. This shortcoming may, however, increase the pleasant surprise that awaits the historian who has not yet realized how much he or she may learn from records that are external to the firm, the subject of the next chapter.

Suggested Readings

The researcher confronted with the need to understand accounting records has several good discussions of the history of accounting to choose from. One of the best is *A History of Accounting Thought* (Hinsdale, Ill.: Dryden Press, 1974) by Michael Chatfield. Another work that may provide insights into accounting in larger firms is *Relevance Lost: The Rise and Fall of Management Accounting* by H. Thomas Johnson and Robert S. Kaplan (Boston, Mass.: Harvard Business School Press, 1987).

The business historian wanting to learn more about the history of advertising has some fascinating reading. Roland Marchand, *Advertising the American Dream: Making Way for Modernity, 1920-1940* (Berkeley and Los Angeles: University of California Press, 1985), has set the standard. Marchand explored the advertising industry in its most important formative years. Michael Schudson, *Advertising, the Uneasy Persuasion* (New York: Basic Books, 1984) is also profound. Daniel Pope, *The Making of Modern Advertising* (New York: Basic Books, 1983) is an interpretive account of the development of advertising as an institution.

Stephen Fox, *The Mirror Makers: A History of American Advertising and Its Creators* (New York: Vintage Books, 1985) is also informative.

The best general history of developments in technology is a two-volume work, *Technology in Western Civilization* edited by Melvin Kranzberg and Carroll Pursell (New York: Oxford University Press, 1967). A second multivolume history by Charles Singer, et. al., *History of Technology* (Oxford: Clarendon Press, 1954-1984), may provide useful information. David Hounshell, *From the American System to Mass Production: the Development of Manufacturing Technology in the United States* (Baltimore: The Johns Hopkins University Press, 1984), will be of value to those persons exploring the history of manufacturing firms. These works contain a wealth of information on specific machines and processes that may help in placing a firm's products or process in context. In addition, the Kranzburg and Pursell history has an extensive bibliography that suggests additional relevant studies.

There are several manuals that clearly explain the techniques of collecting oral history. *Nearby History* by David Kyvig and Myron Marty, the parent volume to this book, contains an excellent discussion of the technique, as does Barbara Allen, *From Memory to History: Using Oral Sources in Local Historical Research* (Nashville, TN.: American Association for State and Local History, 1981). To a considerable degree the success of an interview will depend upon good preparation. It is most important to have contacted the subject in advance and to have in writing an agreement that spells out how the material gathered will be used. The publications of the Oral History Association, as well as Willa K. Baum's *Oral History for the Local Historical Society,* (3rd ed.; Nashville, TN.: American Association for State and Local History, 1987) provide samples of appropriate letters and forms.

·5·

Local Business History— External Sources

OFTEN THE EXPLORATION OF HISTORICAL SOURCES THAT originated outside of the firm becomes an essential part of the local business historian's task. Chapter 3 examined some of the questions about the business firm that the historian ought to raise in order to make an analysis most complete and meaningful to readers. This chapter will explain the sources most commonly used by business historians as they try to place the firm they are studying into a larger setting. Much of the discussion will pertain to information about business generated by agencies of the federal government. Comparable information sources may come from the state government under whose jurisdiction the firm fell, but space is not available to discuss all fifty of those possibilities. This chapter will also point out some helpful private sources of information about individual firms.

As chapter 3 suggested, the business history of greatest interest to readers is the one that illuminates the larger picture of the community's past. Business history like any form of history is most interesting if it is placed in a context that is meaningful in terms larger than the particular case. To accomplish this important goal, the researcher needs to look for sources that exist externally to the firm under study. External sources can be used for more than placing the firm under study in its broader setting, however important that task may be. It is a common experience even for the historian who enjoys a rich lode of internal business sources, such as a well-kept and logically organized company archives, to want to find more information about the firm. There may be significant gaps in the firm's own record keeping. Older materials especially are likely to be sketchy, destroyed by fire or vermin, or casually discarded by an owner or employee who carelessly thought that no one would ever be interested in the records and the activities they represented. These are all good reasons to scrutinize sources of information about the firm that may be found outside of the firm itself.

In carefully considering the possibilities of locating important external sources, the business historian remains ever mindful of paying continuing attention to the firm's internal sources. Any historian, not just a business historian, asks questions concerning what the actors under consideration thought and how their anticipations materialized. The business historian pays attention, thus, to how entrepreneurs and executives considered their business situations, what they did about those situations, and how successful they were in realizing their goals. Internal sources of the firm are desirable for answering those questions. External sources are essential for a whole range of other important questions. How did other persons contemporary to the business observe its behavior? How did business executives and their contemporaries interact with one another, and how did those interactions affect behaviors? Business historians ask how the dynamic workings of the firm under study in the free interplay of market forces affected the strategy and hence the structure of the firm.

In discussing ways to uncover information about a business firm's history, readers should consult the parent volume of this series, *Nearby History*. It is a treasury of helpful, practical suggestions not just on questions that are appropriately raised while a scholar is preparing a history but of reference tools that guide researchers along their paths so that they will uncover the information required. We try to follow a principle in our work as historians of asking questions that are meaningful to us, and hopefully to our readers and students, and then to look for the information required to answer those questions. Sometimes the answers are simply unavailable, but we are frequently pleased to discover that much can be learned from available sources. With its suggestions of both questions to ask and research strategies and techniques to pursue, *Nearby History* suggests the value of the researcher following that principle.

Newer Reference Tools

Since the publication of *Nearby History*, new finding aids and research tools have appeared that may be useful in exploring the local firm's past. No guide such as this one can pretend to remain current for long in the rapidly changing field of information science, but it may suggest some trends to observe in planning a research project. First, the electronic computer has dramatically changed the ways that both librarians and business persons create, file, and access information, and therefore the opportunities for historians to uncover the information they want. One way in which the use of the computer has changed the acquisition of information is through on-line services. On-line services are huge data banks maintained, usually, by commercial firms who charge for accessing them. CD-Rom, which stands for Compact Disk-Read Only Memory, is another way in which business information is being made available through the use of the computer. In any case, today's businesses comprise the largest market for electronically accessed information sources, so business historians in the future will be taking advantage of them more and more for taking up the story of business in the 1970s and beyond.

One other significant prefatory remark needs to be made about using historical sources external to the business firm. Much business information is reported by the Standard Industrial Classification Code, or SICC, a system of classifying business information devised and occasionally updated by the executive branch of the federal government. The scholar exploring a local business is well advised to know the primary code, and any secondary codes, the firm under investigation would be assigned. The United States Technical Committee on Industrial Classification publishes the *Standard Industrial Classification Manual* in which the system is briefly explained, changes noted, and the codes displayed by industry. The usual sources of business information that will be mentioned in this chapter, such as Standard and Poor's, will usually report the SICC for particular firms, and often investor's services, especially those accessed with the aid of an electronic computer, are indexed by the Standard Industrial Classification Code. We have used these codes in an electronic search to pinpoint the names of firms competing with the one whose history we are writing.

As this brief discussion of using the computer as a research tool for finding historical information suggests, librarians have been busy developing new finding aids that greatly help the historian. And historians have completed or embarked on major scholarly reference projects of their own that will better illuminate America's business heritage. These reference tools are essential in planning a business history, and they remain handy as one progresses through the research and writing phases. As the historian studies documents from the past, new questions frequently arise that lead the researcher back again and again to the reference shelves of the library.

Especially important to the historian planning a research project is the *National Inventory of Documentary Sources in the United States.* The *National Inventory* is a valuable reference tool for planning a historical research project in any field, not just in business history, especially when the researcher is unsure about the location of relevant manuscript materials. This reference tool attempts not only to list each of the manuscript collections in the United States (as well as in Great Britain), but it also provides a copy of the finding aid that the archivists have prepared to assist the person conducting research in a particular collection. The *Inventory* is well indexed. However, only the index to federal records has appeared as a printed volume; all other materials are published on microfiche. The historian wishing to explore a local business may use this tool by looking up the name of the individual firm in the indexes, as well as exploring possible sources for the study of the industry of which the firm is a part. After reading the inventory, the researcher may write a more informed letter of inquiry to the repository listed in order to decide if a personal visit is worthwhile, or if funds should be spent to employ a local researcher to photocopy needed information.

The other important general source of information about manuscript collections that may be of interest is the *National Union Catalog of Manuscript Collections,* published by the Library of Congress. This multivolume set is carefully indexed, and is a more complete survey of manuscript collections in the United States than the *National Inventory,* although both reference tools are missing information when depositories failed to notify the compilers of their holdings. NUCMC, however, has much less information about an individual collection than does the *National Inventory.* In any event, searching for information about a firm outside of its own archives requires use of both the *National Inventory* and NUCMC.

Although the *National Inventory of Documentary Sources in the United States* and the *National Union Catalog of Manuscripts Collections* are of general usefulness to all persons wanting to learn more about the availability and location of manuscript materials in government archives, historical societies, and libraries, business historians are fortunate in having a few reference tools specific to the speciality. We frequently consult the more traditional printed guidebooks by Larson and Lovett discussed in chapter 1. (As this volume goes to press, *The Handbook of American Business History,* edited by David O. Whitten, is to be published by the Greenwood Press as a three-volume work; one aim of the *Handbook* is to update the bibliographical listings in Larson and Lovett's valuable guides.) Also, *Information*

Sources in Advertising History, Richard W. Pollay, ed. & comp. (Westport, CT: Greenwood, 1979) is most valuable for the historian exploring a local business who is interested in knowing more about the important subject of advertising. Anyone writing the history of an advertising firm, of course, will want to begin with this valuable reference tool.

Two important biographical projects, the smaller completed and the larger just underway, are important sources of information for business historians. The smaller of the two, John N. Ingham, *Biographical Dictionary of American Business Leaders* (4 vols.; Westport: Greenwood Press, 1983) is a convenient, general reference work containing information on 1,159 individuals, almost all of whom were born in the nineteenth century. There are fifty volumes planned for *The Encyclopedia of American Business History and Biography*. *Railroads in the Age of Regulation,* edited by Keith L. Bryant, Jr. (Vol. I; New York: Facts on File, 1988) and *Railroads in the Nineteenth Century,* edited by Robert L. Frey (Vol. II; New York: Facts on File, 1988) provide a comprehensive coverage of that important industry.

There is one other bibliographical tool that may be of help because it addresses a subject that is closely related to business history. William K. Hutchison, *American Economic History: A Guide to Information Sources* (Detroit: Gale Research, 1980) is indexed by author, title, and subject. This reference volume treats subjects from colonial times to about 1960. The author has annotated some of the entries, adding to its usefulness when embarking on our exploration of the story of a particular firm.

The Federal Government and Business Information

The federal government is a major source of information about business, and its records may provide rich opportunities for the historian of a local firm to acquire needed information. The federal government sources are important to the local historian because business firms have interacted with the federal government often and in important ways since at least 1789. This interaction has increased since the turn of the twentieth century and the growth of what is sometimes called *the regulatory state.* Federal officials have been interested in collecting, analyzing, and disseminating information about business and information useful to the conduct of business, since at least the Census of 1810. Information about business will appear in both published and unpublished forms. Unpublished federal records are most commonly in the custody of the National Archives and Records

Administration, although recent materials of interest to the historian are usually still housed in the agency that produced or received them.

In approaching information sources from the federal government, it is useful to keep in mind the distinctions between the executive, legislative, and judicial branches, along with the independent regulatory commissions. The published materials from each of the branches will be accessed in different ways. Fortunately for the historian, recently developed reference tools have greatly eased the task of insuring a thorough and accurate search pinpointing the subjects of interest. These reference tools are concisely and clearly outlined, including an explanation of how to use them, in Julia Schwartz, *Easy Access to Information in United States Government Documents* (Chicago: American Library Association, 1986).

There are tools of special value to historians in the hunt for information from federal documents. The *Monthly Catalog of United States Government Publications* is a comprehensive listing of the publications of the federal government. The *Monthly Catalog* has a cumulative subject index that covers the years 1895-1899 and 1900-1971. The names of individual companies are sometimes listed in the subject index, and the historian is likely to find references to the industries in which he or she is interested. For all issues there are indexes that go beyond subject listings. In using this and other indexes, researchers, of course, have to remain imaginative in thinking of subject headings, for the language used by the person who prepared the original index may be different from our own. For instance, references to beer and brewing might appear under *malt liquor* because that was a commonly used term when the government began printing its *Monthly Catalog*.

The *Monthly Catalog* lists all federal government publications regardless of the agency from which they originated. Sometimes it is helpful to know more about the agencies themselves. A useful tool for learning more about the executive branch of the federal government is the *United States Government Manual*, printed annually since 1935 by the Government Printing Office. The *Manual*, an official organization handbook, summarizes the duties, programs, structure, and functions of federal agencies, and contains name, subject, and agency indexes. An appendix lists transferred or abolished agencies. Once the agencies of interest have been determined, it is easy to look for annual reports of those agencies to find out about their work. Eventually it may be useful to see if their records in the National Archives will provide helpful information. (This task requires use of the Archives' finding aids, readily reproduced in the *National Inventory of*

Documentary Collections, already discussed earlier in this chapter.) And, of course, there are innumerable special publications by agencies that may have a bearing on a particular firm under study, especially if it was part of an industry that was a special concern of public policy.

For the congressional branch of government, there are superior finding aids that allow the researcher to determine if there are publications pertaining to the industry under study. A private firm, the Congressional Information Service, has published its *CIS/Index* since 1970, which has a detailed summary of congressional hearings, including the names of individual witnesses. Less detailed, but of very high value for the historian, are retrospective volumes of the *CIS/Index* pertaining to congressional publications prior to 1970.

Business issues have comprised much of the nation's courtroom activity, and it is often worthwhile to peruse court decisions and court records. Doing so requires the use of a law library and the special skills of a law librarian that are beyond the purview of this volume. Finding the text of a court decision may well be worth the trouble, however. Judges often write discursively about the case at hand, sometimes even providing a review of the history behind the issues, which they have based on documents supplied by the contending attorneys. The National Archives contains court records pertaining to business.

The National Archives

For the business historian, like other students of the past, the National Archives is a treasure house of unpublished historical data. (Important as published information is, it only comprises a tiny fraction of all federal data.) The location of the Archives and the Library of Congress in Washington, D.C., make that city akin to a mecca for almost any American historian. As one veteran archivist in tune to the needs of business historians, Meyer H. Fishbein, once observed (in "Business History Sources in the National Archives," *Business History Review* 38 (Summer 1964): 232-257), "It may be stated with assurance that the holdings of the National Archives include the largest collection of papers concerning American business in the custody of any institution."

Before visiting the National Archives, however, it is important to plan the research venture there. The records held by the National Archives are vast, with nearly one million cubic feet housed in the main building alone.

The scholar planning to explore the archival records of the federal government will want to begin with the *Guide to the National Archives of the United States* (Washington, D.C.: National Archives and Records Service, 1974). The business historian will also find two essays by experienced archivists helpful. Meyer Fishbein's essay, "Business History Sources in the National Archives," cited above, speaks generally, and, because it has a regional focus, Jerome Finster, "Some Aspects of Federal Archives Relating to New England Businesses Before 1920" in James Lawton, ed., *Shop Talk: Papers on Historical Business and Commercial Records of New England* (Boston: Boston Public Library, 1975) is rewarding for the local historian. Finster, for example, explained that the Archives holds thousands of bankruptcy records from the federal district courts that can be of interest to the business historian. Sometimes the cases are arranged alphabetically; usually, however, the cases are listed numerically with accompanying registers to help locate the records desired. In any event, planning a trip to the National Archives will almost certainly require use of the *National Inventory of Documentary Records* for a careful reading of the agency's finding aid, called a "preliminary inventory." The researcher may obtain a list of Archives' publications by writing to the Publications Division, National Archives, Washington, D.C. 20408. After examining the relevant published finding aids, but before visiting the Archives, one should always write a letter of inquiry concerning the availability of records and their location.

A visit to the National Archives should also be approached with imagination. The institution holds so much material, and the federal government stands as such a labyrinth of agencies, that the historian of a local business will want to think in advance of times and ways in which the firm may have interacted with a government agency. In general, if a local business historian finds a published government report of some sort that seems to pertain to the industry—or even the individual firm—under study, the researcher is well advised to inquire if there are relevant unpublished materials available in the National Archives, or in a state archives if the report was produced by an agency of a state government.

State governments also usually maintain archives. Although it is impossible to review here the research possibilities in each of the fifty states, it may be wise to do so for the state or states in which a firm did business. *Nearby History* lists state historical societies and archives in an appendix. Anyone researching the history of a firm in Virginia is fortunate to have available *A Guide to the Business Records in the Archives Branch, Virginia State*

Tax records, such as this 1902 receipt, can provide insights into what the company owned and its value.

Library (Conley L. Edwards III, comp.; Richmond: Virginia State Library, 1983). For nineteenth-century economic materials that appeared in state government publications, Adelaide R. Hasse, *Index of Economic Material in Documents of the United States* (15 vols.; Washington: Carnegie Institution of Washington, 1907-1922) is invaluable. The volumes are arranged by states, and cover California, Delaware, Illinois, Kentucky, Maine, Massachusetts, New Hampshire, New Jersey, New York, Ohio, Pennsylvania, Rhode Island, and Vermont. The local historian will find printed reports of special state commissions, executive officers, and legislative committees described.

For the local business historian exploring records in the national archives, three agencies may provide unexpected information. *Preliminary Inventory of the Records of the Smaller War Plants Corporation* (Katherine H. Davidson, comp.; Washington: The National Archives, 1964) describes the records of a World War II agency created in 1942 to help place war contracts in small businesses. The Company Case Files of the Agency Contact Division contain correspondence with smaller firms, arranged by the name of the business. For the World War I period, *Preliminary Inventory of the War Industries Board Records* (Washington: The National Archives, 1941) has an index, listing numerous industries and some individual firms, which may guide the researcher to materials of interest. More generally, the Bureau of Foreign and Domestic Commerce was mostly concerned with foreign trade matters. The National Archives contain 847 feet of this bureau's general records from the period 1914-1958, materials which the researcher may access from a 26-foot card index, arranged by subjects in alphabetical order.

As this chapter will point out further, the National Archives houses many more types of records that the local historian may wish to consult. But the Archives is not the only federal agency to which the business historian may turn in search of information about a particular business.

The Securities and Exchange Commission and Investor Services

The Securities and Exchange Commission, created by Congress in 1934 to regulate the nation's stock exchanges, is often an important source of information for the business historian concerned with developments after the middle of the 1930s. In fact, the reports from publicly held firms collected by the SEC provide information that investors rely upon in reaching financial decisions. The spirit of the federal regulation of the securities industry is self-disclosure. Thus the SEC requires publicly held companies to file reports regularly. These reports contain information similar to that found in the firm's own annual report to the stockholders, and often they are more valuable than the annual report because the information is not clouded with public relations devices. Business writers often use the category of SEC reports as their own shorthand. Companies must file an annual report with the SEC, commonly called a 10-K report. They also submit information quarterly, commonly called the 10-Q report. Finally, there is the Report of Unscheduled Material Events or Corporate Changes, commonly called the 8-K report, that posts notifications of impending mergers and the like that might affect the vitality of the firm.

Gaining access to the disclosure statements poses special problems to the historian that investors may not encounter, simply because historians are always interested in the perspectives that long runs of information provide. Nevertheless, services developed to assist investors may offer aid. First, the Securities and Exchange Commission publishes a directory of the firms reporting to it where the researcher can look up the firm or firms of interest. The *Directory of Companies Required to File Annual Reports with the Securities and Exchange Commission*, available from the Government Printing Office and in research libraries, has been issued annually by the Commission since

1976. As for the reports themselves, in the past they were too bulky for libraries to keep, but now the reports are published on microfiche and are more available in libraries. The reports may also be consulted on microfiche at the SEC office in Washington, D.C., and in the Commission's offices in New York, Chicago, and Los Angeles. Other regional offices may have copies of the reports. An individual may order any report directly from the SEC. Address inquiries to the Public Reference Section, Securities and Exchange Commission, Washington, D.C. 20549. The telephone number is (202) 272-7450.

The historian is, of course, interested in reports extending back into time, and observing trends in both the financial data and the comments supplied by top corporate officials. Older reports may be found in records housed in the National Archives. The *Preliminary Inventory of the Records of the Securities and Exchange Commission* (Herbert J. Horwitz, comp.; Washington: National Archives, 1964) is the Archives' guide to its holdings. The SEC records consist of over one thousand feet of manuscript materials, accessed by a card index that occupies four feet. These materials are the registration dossiers and related records of publicly traded companies filing reports with the SEC. The materials for each firm—prospectuses, periodic financial reports, and the like—are grouped together. These materials may be an excellent starting place for the historian of a local business about which it is difficult to obtain basic, reliable information from other sources.

Although not a source of information obtained from the federal government directly, persons doing research about business rely heavily on information from public reference services that do obtain data from the SEC reports. These investment reference services are commonly found even in smaller public libraries. They seldom contain much historical information, however, although they are sometimes a useful starting point for seeking information about a particular firm. Lorna M. Daniells, *Business Information Sources* (rev. ed.; Berkeley: University of California Press, 1985) is the standard guide to turn to again and again on many subjects, including the investor's reference services.

Each person may have a favorite investor's reference service, but *Moody's Industrial Manual* published by Moody's Investors Service in New York can be especially useful to the historian because it is available on microfiche from 1909. This reference is a source of financial information about individual firms. It also sometimes provides a brief history of the firm, as well as contemporary information about its facilities and officers. The Standard

and Poor's Corporation in New York is another publisher of popular investor's services. Its *Daily News* and *Cumulative News* are available on-line from
September, 1979. This source includes financial news on leading firms,
news of mergers and management changes, and financial statements. Investor's information in general is also available from on-line and CD-ROM services, and the researcher may wish to ask a reference specialist in a business
library for assistance.

There are some special sources of news about the securities markets
(stocks and bonds) that business historians sometimes find useful. The
Commercial and Financial Chronicle, which has been published in New York
City for well over a century, is especially important to the business historian
looking for nineteenth-century information. The main purpose of the
Chronicle, which was issued weekly, was the publication of daily bond and
stock prices. This information may be available for regional exchanges as
well as the New York Stock Exchange. The magazine also published some
news articles about business, but in the absence of a comprehensive index,
they can be difficult to locate. For more recent times, the *Wall Street Transcript* has published weekly beginning in 1963, and is available on microfilm. Each issue is indexed, and the films include the accumulated quarterly
indexes. For issues beginning in July of 1981, the information may be accessed through the on-line service, VuText. The *Transcript* reprints the text
of selected brokerage house reports on firms and industries. It also publishes
interviews with business leaders and reports the remarks made by company
executives to the group informally known as "Wall Street analysts," the persons employed by brokerage firms to follow the trends of industries and companies.

Business historians want to know what other actors—entrepreneurs, executives, brokers, investors, and the like—observed about the firm they are
studying. An important source of information about a company and the industry in which it operates may be the research reports of the brokerage
houses. Traditionally these reports were made available to investors who
used the brokerage firm to handle their securities transactions, and to the
individual brokers to aid them in advising their clients. Regrettably, we
know of no brokerage house that maintains an archive of their reports.
Many of these reports became available to general researchers in 1983.
(Regrettably, reports written before 1983 are usually unavailable.) Larger
university and public libraries may subscribe to the *Corporate and Industry
Research Reports* (Eastchester, NY: J.A. Micropublishing), a microfiche

publication with annual printed indexes. The usefulness of this source depends on the publisher's success in obtaining permission to reproduce research reports.

The Federal Censuses and Business

The federal censuses provide local historians in many fields with otherwise unobtainable information for their quests. This is no less true for the business historian than for the genealogist or family historian. The federal census is a rich pool of information for the local historian wanting to learn more about a nearby business and the context of the firm's operations.

The main historical source of business information is the Census of Manufactures. The decennial census of the United States began collecting business information in 1810. Criticism of the inadequacy and inaccuracy of earlier information led Congress to provide for the collection of more complete information beginning with the 1850 census. In its Schedule 5 for 1850 the government tried to collect information about the firms that were producing articles valued at least at $500 per year. The census schedules that the bureau's employees took with them into the field called for information on fourteen categories, starting with the name of the business and its products. The information gained from the census of 1850 may provide the local business historian with a starting point, although some investigators have found the information reported often incomplete. The *Compendium of the Seventh Census* of 1850 reported figures by county for capital invested, number of persons (called *hands* in the nineteenth-century language) employed, and the value of product, information that may provide an immediate context into which to place information about a particular firm. Based on her research on economic history of Wisconsin in the mid-nineteenth century, Margaret Walsh recommended that the historian rely on the manuscript census schedules, not the printed compilations of them, for local history. "On a local level these records contain gross errors and deficiencies which could result in the misinterpretation of facts," she warned in "The Value of Mid-Nineteenth Century Manufacturing Returns: The Printed Census and the Manuscript Census Compilations Compared," *Historical Methods Newsletter*, 4 (March 1971): 43.

The census began surveying manufacturing in 1810, upon Congress' request. Partly this action stemmed from concern for the impact of the Napoleonic wars on the importation of European manufactured goods. From

1849 to 1899 the Census of Manufactures occurred every ten years, and it covered building trades and neighborhood industries as well as factories. The census of 1860 was the first to publish a separate volume on manufacturers, *Eighth Census, 1860, Manufactures*, vol. III. From 1904 to 1919, the Census of Manufactures occurred every five years, and covered only the factory system—establishments whose products were worth more than $500. From 1921 to 1939 it was taken every two years, now excluding firms whose products were valued less than $5000. During World War II the biennial censuses were suspended. Finally, in 1947 the Census of Manufactures covered all firms. Beginning in 1949 the Census of Manufactures was taken annually.

The published volumes of the census can provide the business historian with some unexpected help. Before 1890, census officials analyzed their data in written essays, and the censuses contain rarely cited industrial histories. After 1890, however, the trade press had grown to the point where census officials no longer felt it necessary for the government to provide commentaries on the data collected, although the Census Bureau published an occasional essay in the early twentieth century. Meyer H. Fishbein describes contemporary commentaries in some depth in "The Censuses of Manufacturers: 1810-1890," *National Archives Accessions—Supplement to the National Archives Guide* (June, 1963).

The Census Bureau has a much shorter tradition of collecting business information on types of establishments not classified as manufacturing. Nevertheless, for the twentieth century especially the information compiled in the census can aid in the exploration of a local business. The federal government only began collecting systematic business information on the retail, service, and wholesale trades in 1929. There were further such censuses taken in 1933, 1935, 1939, and 1948. Beginning in 1954 there was to be such a census taken every five years, to be called the Census of Business. The Census Bureau has compiled and published these data by local area, providing the historian exploring a local business an opportunity to place the particular firm into a larger yet still local context. If he or she is investigating the history of a drug store, for instance, these data will make it possible to determine how many such stores there were in a county or city, and to assess how many of them over the years operated soda fountains. With its first edition published in 1949, and periodically updated, the Census Bureau has provided a *County and City Data Book*, which allows the local business historian of recent times a ready statistical source with which to place the firm under study in its local context. This source provides information about the wholesale and retail trades, selected service industries, including banking, and employment by manufacturers, as well as population characteristics of cities and counties.

The National Archives houses some of the business data collected in the various censuses. *The Preliminary Inventory of the Records of the Bureau of the Census* (Catherine H. Davidson and Charlotte M. Ashby, comps.; Washington: National Archives, 1964) indicates that most of the census of manufactures schedules were disposed of by the National Archives. But that disposal does not mean that the records were destroyed. When Congress in 1918–1919 authorized their disposal, the schedules for the 1850–1880 period were transferred to non-federal depositories, usually a state historical society or library. There the schedules of the Census of Manufactures might still be found. Since the establishment of the National Archives, there has been a partly successful effort to have the Archives obtain microfilm copies of those census schedules. And potentially valuable information remains available for the researcher in the National Archives. The historian exploring a local business may find information in the National Archives for 1931 and 1933; the schedules are filed, first, by standard industrial code numbers, and, second, alphabetically by firm name for each state. Similarly, manuscript schedules are available for the 1929 Census of Distribution and the 1935 Census of Business, the latter available only on microfilm.

Federal Agencies and Local Business

As chapter 3 observed, the federal government began regulating business through special regulatory agencies beginning with the creation of the Interstate Commerce Commission in 1887. The Securities and Exchange Commission, already discussed as a source of information for the business historian, is one example of a regulatory agency. Just as the researcher may obtain information directly from the SEC, so too may he or she find it necessary to work directly with another regulatory agency—even if some of its records are on deposit in the National Archives.

The original regulatory agency, the Interstate Commerce Commission, might prove a valuable source of transportation-related information about a firm. The costs of moving freight were vitally important to American manufacturing firms, and someone studying the history of a local manu-

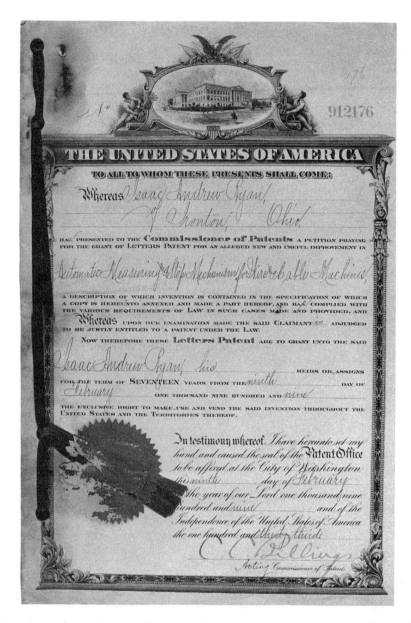

Patent documents provide a record of innovations that a company or its workers have made. While such documents are important sources of information about the technology, they should not be used as the only source of technical data since many improvements were not patented.

facturer may be interested especially in materials relating to the regulation of those costs. The Interstate Commerce Commission followed regular procedures regarding its overview of freight rates that sometimes involved the holding of extensive hearings in Washington, D.C., and the publication of decisions much as courts do. Voluminous transcripts of the hearings of largest national significance are still retained by the ICC. Permission to see them is not automatic, however. Requests should be directed to The Secretary, Interstate Commerce Commission, Washington, D.C. 20423. The telephone number of the ICC's library is (202) 275-7423. Individual commissioners also travelled to local areas to hear about concerns regarding freight rates, but those events were less formal and the local researcher is unlikely to discover them.

The Federal Trade Commission, founded by Congress in 1914 and modelled on the ICC to some extent, may be of interest to the local historian. Supplanting the Bureau of Corporations that began in 1903, the FTC held a mandate to provide a kind of general overview of American business, especially regarding unfair trade practices that might result in antitrust actions. Both the bureau and the commission have conducted numerous investigations of businesses over the years. Some of those records might not be open to the business historian, however, because the investigations involved confidential, proprietary information. Generally, however, the files of FTC investigations of particular complaints are open to the public. The commission staff assigned each investigation of particular complaints against a company a docket number, and the National Archives has the records filed under that docket number. The researcher may obtain the docket number only by a systematic search of the published *Federal Trade Commission Reports*, each volume of which has an index. {If there is doubt about gaining access to FTC records, the researcher may approach the commission itself for permission to use some of its materials, which are still considered to be confidential, by writing to the Secretary, Federal Trade Commission, Washington, D.C. 20580. The telephone number of the FTC's Public Reference Branch is (202) 523-3598.}

The finding aids of the National Archives regarding FTC records will not direct the researcher to the docket number regarding investigations of particular firms, but they may help locate records pertaining to broader investigations. The archives of the FTC materials and their method of filing are described in *Preliminary Inventory of the Records of the Federal Trade Commission* (Estelle Rebec, comp.; Washington: National Archives, 1948). The

When government regulation eliminated narcotics in patent medicines, the family that owned the Peruna, a best-selling nostrum, invested capital in a substantial commercial farm, here photographed in the late 1930s.

materials in the National Archives include index files to those investigations, files which will have the names of individual companies. The researcher may learn about the earlier investigations of the Federal Trade Commission by consulting the *Annual Report of the Federal Trade Commission for the Fiscal Year Ended June 30, 1938*, pp. 173-193, which lists all of the FTC's investigations to that date, with a concise description of each.

In his pathbreaking study of the relationship between the development of large and small businesses in the United States, *Small Enterprise and Oligopoly: A Study of the Butter, Flour, Automobile, and Glass Container Industries,* published by Oregon State College in 1955, Harold Vatter found the use of federal government records, especially those of the Federal Trade Commission, essential. Primarily from these records—not from company records, which were mainly closed to him—Vatter was able to reconstruct the historical development of the companies in the industries in which he was interested and the changing relationships of the companies to one another.

For instance, investigations made by the Federal Trade Commission in 1920 into the flour industry revealed clearly the growth of concentration in that industry. The commission's *Report on Commercial Wheat Flour Milling* (Washington, September 15, 1920) showed that "In the ten years from 1904 to 1914 . . . one out of every three mills having an annual output of 5,000 to 20,000 barrels went out of business . . . [while] the number of mills making over 100,000 barrels increased from 166 to 218, their output amounting to over 60 percent of the total for the entire country." The report attributed this growing concentration largely to technological innovations in grinding the grain which, in turn, created economies of scale and encouraged the development of big mills.

The Securities and Exchange Commission, as explained, requires reports from corporations whose securities are traded either over the counter at brokerage houses or on a stock exchange. But what if the local firm under investigation is not publicly held? Federal agencies may still provide you with information needed to prepare a full history. Even privately held firms may have to report business information about themselves to federal agencies. This reporting will be true especially as they touch upon regulatory agencies, or other federal agencies whose purpose is to aid businesses in various ways. Christine Flint and Stephen M. Conway, eds., *The Company Data Directory* (Washington: Research Counsel of Washington, 1983) is an invaluable tool for the scholar who wants to discover information from federal agencies. *The Company Data Directory* suggests agencies that may have information about a particular firm because that firm, although privately held, must inform the agencies because of some dealing it has with the federal government. For instance, a privately held barge company might have to report information to the federal agencies controlling the country's interior waterways, or to the Interstate Commerce Commission. A privately held manufacturer who enjoys contracts from the Department of Defense may have information about itself on file in a Pentagon office. In fact, contracts going back to 1789 might be found in the records of several agencies.

Gaining access to such information can be difficult at best, however. It may be necessary to use the procedures provided in the Freedom of Information Act, first passed in 1966, and amended thereafter. Congress intended the law to provide procedures for citizens to obtain information from their government, but investigators nevertheless sometimes experience difficulty with recalcitrant federal officials. If Freedom of Information procedures need to be used, it is best to consult specialized publications. *The Company Data Directory* includes tips on how to use the law's procedures. A short pamphlet prepared for a professional society is David A. Trask, David M. Baehler, and Roger M. Anders, *User's Guide to the Freedom of Information Act* (Bloomington, Indiana: Organization of American Historians, 1984); it can be obtained from the OAH at 112 North Bryan St., Bloomington, IN 47401. This pamphlet includes forms to use in requesting information, which the authors adapted from a congressional committee report.

Viewing the Firm from Private Sources

There are several important ways that business historians may wish to view the firm they are exploring from sources that are neither from a governmental agency nor from the firm's records themselves. There are, of course, countless general, private sources available to the researcher, who is guided to them best by *Nearby History*. There are as well some sources that are fairly specialized to business history.

Business executives are necessarily concerned with credit, banking, and financial information of many sorts. Business historians can use for their own purposes the information developed to guide executives in these important areas. Of most interest is information gathered about a particular firm by other businesses who may be considering it as a credit risk. Information about individual business firms and individual business entrepreneurs is important to banks and other lending agencies. The nineteenth century saw the development of private credit reporting services. James H. Madison, "The Evolution of Commercial Credit Reporting Agencies in Nineteenth-Century America, *Business History Review,* 48 (Summer 1974), 164-186 is a worthwhile account of the general phenomenon of the growth of credit agencies that serviced the needs of American business.

Fortunately for the business historian, the records of the pioneer credit reporting firm, R. G. Dun & Co., of New York, now part of Dun & Bradstreet, are available to us in the Baker Library of the Harvard Business School. The R. G. Dun & Co., the first commercial credit reporting agency in the United States, traced its history to 1841. The firm flourished by the 1850s when it was employing 2000 correspondents in the United States and Canada who reported information on individual businessmen to headquarters in New York. There clerks entered the information in ledger books, arranged by county. James H. Madison, "The Credit Reports of R. G. Dun and Co. as Historical Sources," *Historical Methods Newsletter* 8 (1975):128-131 provides a short yet detailed summary of what the business historian will find in the 2,850 ledger books the firm has placed on deposit in the Baker Library. Robert W. Lovett, while serving as the librarian responsible for these records, discussed them in "Nineteenth-Century Credit Information," James Lawton, ed., *Shop Talk: Papers on Historical Business and Commercial Records of New England* (Boston: Boston Public Library, 1975).

Business historians have found the ledger book entries of the R. G. Dun & Co. a rich resource, one that is especially valuable to the local historian because the information is reported by town and firm. The R. G. Dun & Co. had to supply reasonably accurate information in order to survive in the marketplace. Each correspondent usually attempted to supply information about the subject's occupation and net worth, and often supplied personal information that included estimates of the subject's character. The information is most complete for the 1850s, 1860s, and 1870s and may be an ideal source for the local historian trying to uncover information about an individual whose business career included those decades. Other local sources may be more prone to boosterism than were the Dun correspondents, whose success depended on accurate estimates. Larger businesses, of course, were more likely to be rated than were smaller businesses. One word of caution is in order: researchers have found the records filled with abbreviations that may take some time and patience to decipher.

The R. G. Dun & Co. records at Harvard University are in manuscript form, but the firm and its rivals also published extensive reports in the nineteenth century. The first credit reporter to print reports was John M. Bradstreet (his firm eventually merged with Dun to form today's Dun & Bradstreet) who began publishing *Bradstreet's Book of Commercial Reports* in 1857. Bradstreet's *Reports* were explicit ratings and judgments about individual firms and business men. Information in them appeared with numerical codes, each number referring to a standard phrase such as "making money."

Responding to Bradstreet's competition, Dun & Co. began to publish its *The Mercantile Agency's Reference Books* in 1859. The first volume rated 20,268 firms in 519 pages, including indexes. The firms were listed alphabetically by town and state, making this a useful reference. By the end of the Civil War Dun's *Reference Book* began supplying more statistical information about a firm's capital worth, information that other firms could use to make their own objective assessments. Part of the change meant that Dun was no longer just reporting on credit, but was actually supplying credit references. By the end of the 1870s Dun's *Reference Book* was carrying reports from about 10,000 correspondents on over 700,000 firms; by 1900 the number of firms listed exceeded 1,285,000. By the latter part of the nineteenth century Dun was also classifying firms according to 24 categories, a practice that continued until the Standard Industrial Classification Codes of the federal government replaced the system. Dun also began supplying information about the banking and railroad services available in each town for which firms were listed.

Research in newspapers is an activity in which business historians often engage. Newspapers can be a valuable source of information about a particular firm, although the absence of indexes will frustrate the local historian. *The Wall Street Journal* is a nationally circulated daily newspaper aimed at the business executive. An index to it begins in 1955 and includes listings by firm name. Researchers wishing to access the *Journal* from an on-line service may do so for articles published from June, 1979. The Dow Jones Free Text Search is an on-line service providing on-line access to the full text of the *Journal*, *Barron's*, and the Dow Jones News Service. Although it is not a specialized business tool for the business historian, no

American historian can work without using *The New York Times*, which has prided itself for many years in serving as a newspaper of record for the nation. Its index begins with 1851, and serves as a ready reference for specific dates, which the researcher may then use to try to locate material of interest in a local newspaper. Occasionally the local historian will be pleasantly surprised to find an index to a local or regional newspaper of interest. Employees of the Works Progress Administration sometimes did this work in the 1930s, and an inquiry at a local library or historical society is always in order. For instance, there is a WPA index of the *Akron Beacon Journal* that has been distributed on microfilm.

In the future, historians will be able more easily to use local newspapers. Thanks to the ability of the computer to help with the indexing process, many more newspapers have recently been indexed, although without retrospective efforts historians find them of limited value. Nevertheless, an important reason for the indexing is to gain access to business information. There are on-line services that provide for searches in regional newspapers and which may thus be especially important for the local historian, although, again, the retrospective material we want is not available.

Pursuing research in magazines may also be desirable. The *Business Periodicals Index* began publication in 1958 and is especially useful for its thorough coverage of magazines specifically oriented toward business. There is nothing comparable to the *Business Periodicals Index* available for coverage of business magazines before 1958. The *Industrial Arts Index*, which began publication in 1918, is very useful although its emphasis is on technology.

Trade associations, as already discussed, are an important part of the business scene in America during the twentieth century. Much can be learned about what is occurring in a firm's industry by looking at the trade association or associations pertaining to that industry. The historian exploring a local business may learn more about the trade associations to which the firm may have belonged by consulting a directory. *National Trade and Professional Associations of the United States and Canada* (Washington, D.C.: Columbia Books, annual) is an alphabetical listing. For a listing of all types of associations by broad subject categories, geographical districts, and the names of executives, researchers can consult the *Encyclopedia of Associations* (Detroit: Gale Research, biennial).

Trade associations publish newsletters and magazines for their members, the exploration of which will aid the historian of a local firm in relating a company's operations to those of its industry. In addition to learning about these publications from the firm's own files or from the listing of the trade association, there are at least two helpful guides. *Ulrich's International Periodicals Directory* (New York: R.R. Bowker, biennial) is a list, by subject, of thousands of periodicals. A guide that helps advertisers may also help historians. *Standard Rate & Data Service: Business Publication Rates and Data*, published monthly, lists, and indexes alphabetically, American trade journals grouped by industry.

Trade associations themselves often compile and publish statistics about their industry, information that the historian of a local firm will often find useful. These volumes are far too numerous to list here. One example, however, is the United States Brewers' Association's *The Brewing Industry in the United States: Brewers Almanac*, published annually. Although books such as this *Almanac* are handy sources of information, the researcher should remain aware that often the purpose of the publication is to cast the industry in a favorable light. An independent scholar may desire additional information. The *Brewers Almanac*, for instance, gives historical data about per capita beer consumption but not per capita of the drinking age population, which are the figures historians most prize.

Finally, the merger movement has had a deep impact on American business. Mergers sometimes create difficulties for sorting out a company's name and owner. A historian wishing to trace the ownership of a particular firm can consult *Who Owns Whom, North America* (18th ed.; London: Dun and Bradstreet, Ltd.,1986), which is a guide to the ownership of subsidiary companies, with an explanation of how the subsidiary fits into its parent group. This is an especially useful tool for the business historian just beginning his or her adventure, for the ownership of some firms has changed many times thanks to the merger frenzies that have overtaken American business. Because mergers have been such a common phenomenon in the 1980s, the local historian may want to explore the business press for recent information of what was occurring.

Obtaining Reference Assistance

These comments and suggestions about ways and means of obtaining needed information from sources external to the firm whose history is being prepared cannot be concluded without stressing the importance of working actively with reference specialists in libraries, archives, and historical societies. In university and public libraries, historical societies and archives large and small, no one knows the local collections of historical materials better than the librarian or archivist who works with them on a regular basis. Experienced librarians and archivists who know the resources of the institutions in which they work are often able to suggest places to look for information that would not otherwise occur to a historian. They have encountered other researchers and can draw upon knowledge gained from helping them in their tasks. And they usually are professionals in their own right who enjoy resolving mysteries by helping others uncover needed information. Sometimes repositories of historical materials are sadly underfunded and therefore unable to catalog their materials fully and notify the compilers of reference tools of the availability of their materials. Thus only personal contact will provide access to records.

This personal contact might occur even before arrival at the library or archives. In planning a visit to a distant repository, it is best to begin a research relationship with reference specialists by telephone or, better, by letter. Such letters should communicate several matters. The larger project should be succinctly but clearly described. The expected accomplishment of the research visit should be explained so that the local reference specialist may indicate whether it is worthwhile to make the visit. The dates of a planned visit should be noted to insure that the agency will be open. And advice on local hotel and transportation accommodations might be sought, since the experience of previous travelers may be helpful.

In any case, exploring the resources for historical research of other institutions can mean a great deal of excitement and satisfaction and even fun.

·6·

Presenting Local Business History

BUSINESS HAS LONG BEEN CENTRAL TO THE AMERICAN experience. "Business is the very soul of an American," wrote Francis Grund in 1837, "he pursues it, not as a means for procuring himself and his family the necessary comforts of life, but as the fountain of all human felicity." As this statement suggests, the significance of business to the lives and thoughts of Americans makes it important to study the historical development of business in the United States. Individual work will, of course, provide personal satisfaction, but the results may have value to the public as well, which is one reason this volume has stressed the need to see a study as a part of the larger patterns of history. There are three major ways to reach others with the results of a study—through writing about it, through the teaching of business history, and through displays in museums and other public places.

Researching and Writing Business History

Business history has existed for sixty years as a field for research and writing in the United States. The study of history in America emerged as an increasingly professionalized discipline in the late nineteenth and early twentieth centuries. As specialization occurred, business history, together with labor history and agricultural history, grew up as subfields within economic history. Business history first won recognition as a distinct academic discipline with the appointment of N. S. B. Gras as the Straus Professor of Business History at the Harvard Business School in 1928. Gras emphasized

the importance of writing business biographies, company histories analyzing the development of individual big businesses in America.

   Gras's approach dominated the study of business history for a generation.
Such able scholars as Ralph and Muriel Hidy, in their study of the Standard
Oil Company, a book discussed in chapter 2 and worth perusing for its approach to the preparation of a company history, typified this way of doing
research and writing in business history. Company histories have been important building blocks upon which the discipline of business history has
been built, and they remain a very significant thread in the development of
business history today. The preparation of a company history is one means
by which to contribute to the continuing evolution of the field today. As
chapter 2 indicated, we still know too little about some types of businesses,
especially family businesses and small businesses.

   Nonetheless, by the 1940s and 1950s, some scholars were criticizing
what they viewed as the narrowness of this approach and were trying to
broaden the scope of business history. This ferment focused at Harvard University. Influenced by work in economics, anthropology, and sociology,
budding business historians met to discuss matters at Harvard's Research
Center in Entrepreneurial History between 1948 and 1958. From these discussions came attempts to rethink the meaning and purpose of business history. The work of Alfred D. Chandler, Jr., has been of the greatest
significance. Chandler has pioneered in the "institutional" approach to
business history. In his three most important books, *Strategy and Structure*,
The Visible Hand, and *Scale and Scope* discussed in chapter 2, Chandler
moved beyond case studies of individual firms to generalize about the evolution of business institutions.

   The continuing influence of disciplines beyond business history and the
growing efforts to connect business history with American history in general have been apparent in the work of scholars contributing to what has
become known as the "organizational synthesis" of modern American history. As its label suggests, this synthesis, first named by Louis Galambos in
1970, involves the conceptualization of American history in terms of the
growing organization of life and thought. As Galambos has explained,
scholars working in American history have come to see the growth of national organizations beginning in the mid-nineteenth century as marking a
major watershed or turning point in the history of the United States.

   While their work varies in subject and emphasis, historians contributing
to this new synthesis share certain premises. One is the assumption that

some of the most (if not the single most) important changes that have occurred in modern America have centered around the shift from small-scale,
informal, locally or regionally oriented groups to large-scale, national,
formal organizations. The new organizations are characterized by a bureaucratic structure of authority. This shift in organization cuts across traditional boundaries of political, economic, and social history.

Like Chandler's institutional approach, the organizational synthesis involves understanding American history in terms of the development of organizations—political parties, labor unions, professional associations, and
farmers' cooperatives, as well as big businesses. In writing an individual history, it is worthwhile to ask to what degree the company and industry being
studied participated in this fundamental transformation of American life. It
may be, the organizational synthesis notwithstanding, that the particular
company, especially if it is a family firm or a small business, has not been
fully involved in the changes written about by Galambos and others of his
school of thought.

In fact, the organizational synthesis has come under attack by some historians in recent years. These critics claim that the organizational synthesis
has in its description of the modern world "an unmistakable aura of in-
evitability, a sense that, in its broad outlines at least, what has happened
had to happen." Critics also assert that the organizational synthesis does
not allow enough room in history to protest movements and to people not
belonging to organized groups; it thus "consigns the experiences of vast segments of society to the periphery of historical analysis, and in the end,
leaves incomplete our view of modern America," they say. While we think
that the organizational synthesis captures well a central tendency of organization, bureaucratization, and centralization in the American past in general and in business history in particular, we agree on the need to maintain
critical scrutiny. Throughout this volume we have urged the placing of the
history of a company in the full context of developments in its community.
Try to avoid preparing a narrow, internal history.

Organizations and institutions provide America's business historians
with forums where they can present new ideas. The field's major journal,
the *Business History Review,* first appeared in 1927 and is now published
quarterly by Harvard University. The *Review* carries articles, book reviews,
and news of current research and writing in business history. Business history also has two national conferences each year. The most well-established
is the Business History Conference, which began holding an annual

meeting in 1954. In 1975, a number of younger scholars formed a new organization, the Economic and Business Historical Society, which also sponsors an annual conference. At these two conferences historians present papers about their research and exchange ideas on topics in business history.

Once finished with research and writing, most historians want to share their discoveries and ideas with others. One common method of doing this is to publish the findings as a book or as a journal article. There are several ways to do this.

Most state historical societies sponsor the publication of a magazine dealing with the history of their state. To publish an article about a company, contact the editor of the appropriate journal to see if he or she would be interested in reviewing the work for possible publication. If so, send in a copy of the article to the journal. National history journals such as the *Business History Review* might also be interested; again, start by contacting the editor. In any case, scholarly journals usually print instructions for the submission of articles somewhere in each issue.

Another goal may be to publish the findings as a book, a more complicated undertaking. A company whose history has been prepared may subsidize publication by a commercial press or publishing house. Or, if it has the facilities, the company might publish it internally. Alternatively, a university press or the press of a historical society may be approached about publication prospects. It is best to write the editor of the press a cover letter of introduction and explanation of the research. The editor should also receive a five-to-ten-page prospectus or summary of the work. An interested editor will then request the submission of the entire manuscript for review.

History journals, university presses, and the presses of historical societies want to review a work before agreeing to publish it (and, of course, they may decline to publish it). They may agree to publish the work as submitted, but more commonly they may require changes or revisions to make the work clearer and more useful to readers. Editors will make their decisions based upon their own judgments and upon the advice of expert outside readers, usually historians who have knowledge of the topic.

Teaching and Public Presentations of Business History

Business history can be taken to the public through teaching as well as through research and writing. Over the past decade or so, there has been a growing interest in the humanities and history on the part of some businesses and business executives. This broadened interest has been reflected in a growing desire of faculty members at university and college business schools to have their students exposed to those subjects. There has been a considerable increase in the teaching of business history, and especially in the teaching of courses designed for business students, in the 1980s.

Although you may not yourself teach courses in business history, the work you are doing on a company's history may contribute to the teaching efforts of others. Teaching business history depends, of course, on the availability of materials for faculty members to use in preparing their classes. Books and articles based upon research become the basis for lectures in business history courses and are essential for the advancement of teaching in this field.

Public presentations of many sorts are another way to offer the results of research to the public. People are often very interested in lectures and presentations of various sorts on the business history of their communities. Talking to business groups, audiences at public libraries and churches, and with school children can be satisfying experiences, in which it is possible to learn new things or see history from a new angle as a result of the comments from members of the audiences. It is most rewarding to take advantage of the opportunities to share findings with others.

Educational Displays of Business History

Yet another way to make use of investigations in business history is through a museum exhibit. Since the history of a business often offers a convenient window through which to explore a period in the life of a community, it may be an excellent topic for a historical society exhibit, or for an exhibit in some other public place, such as the lobby of a firm's headquarters. The history of a company provides a convenient theme, one that is local and that allows the introduction of broader topics and in many instances one that may be presented effectively through objects and graphics. An examination of the founders and later leaders of a prominent business may provide an opportunity to discuss a community's elite. Analysis of the workforce at a factory may provide an effective way to deal with the importance of immigration, mechanization, and labor unions to a community. A look at a firm's marketing strategies and sources of raw materials may allow an examination of its relationships with other communities.

This c. 1920 view along Union Street in Nashville, Tennessee, shows a typical group of small retail businesses at a time when the center of town was the commercial district.

In the mid-1950s, for example, Olin Mathieson and Revere Copper constructed an aluminum reduction plant near Woodsfield, Ohio, a rural community on the Ohio River. Thirty years later the local historical society and the *Monroe County Beacon*, a weekly newspaper, devoted an expanded issue to the history of the plant. Aside from the inherently interesting story of the business, researchers found that the development and later operations of the plant could, in large measure, tell the recent history of their community.

The aluminum factory attracted over 1000 workers from the South, thus setting in motion a migration that not only brought new people but which in time led to the transplantation of new institutions. For instance, the workers established several new churches. As the population grew, there was a boom in home construction, a need for new schools, revisions to the local highway system, and the founding of many new businesses. Within a few years Woodsfield found that its relationship with the outside world was changing. The price of aluminum became important news. As the factory changed in ownership, mergers and leveraged buyouts became the subjects of articles in the town's weekly newspaper and the topics for discussion at meetings of local service clubs. EPA pollution regulations attracted hundreds of residents to public meetings and became issues in local elections. Strikes at times divided the community, and the cycle of labor contracts was of importance to local merchants.

In a word, the life of one business came to dominate that community so completely that the local historical society could tell a substantial part of the area's history by using the business as a focal point. Besides being a very useful way of organizing the region's history, using the business as a focal point brought support to the historical society. The firm and the individual workers contributed artifacts and funds to the society's efforts. While not every community will have a dominant firm, almost all have important businesses that can provide valuable insights into the histories of their communities. In most instances, firms will not only cooperate, but will be pleased to support efforts to tell their stories through exhibits that will be made available to broad audiences.

Audiovisual presentations are yet another medium through which business history can be set forth. They may take the forms of slide lectures, films, or videotapes. A slide show and talk can be an effective means of offering history to school classes, service clubs, and employee and management groups. With a well-stocked image library and a good understanding of a firm's history, it is possible to tailor presentations to specific audiences and easily update them as desired. A slide lecture is also a good intermediate step to either a published history or museum exhibit. Slide presentations may encourage people to share information and often stimulate interest that can be capitalized upon when the book or exhibit is completed.

The recent advent of community-access television and the widespread availability of video equipment provide a forum for researchers who can use video cameras. The videotape shares an important characteristic with the slide show: both media allow people who under normal circumstances would not read a book to become familiar with the subject.

Commercial or public television and radio stations in a community may take an active interest in presenting information on local history. The historian of a local business may find an interest in the electronic media either as a special feature, or a segment in a regular news program. In some cases there is a particular producer who enjoys a historical interest, or a reporter

This photograph was a source for a large display in the History Mall of the Ohio Historical Society.

who regularly receives assignments to cover historical topics. You may want to make your work known to that person, keeping in mind that television producers will probably desire visual images, and radio stations sound recordings to incorporate in the report.

There may be an outlet for historical work in articles published in the local newspaper. The work may have to be serialized. Serialization requires special attention to organization so that each chapter can stand on its own. Like audiovisual media, newspaper serials reach wide audiences. Newspaper serials have the additional advantage of being an inexpensive way of presenting research and of obtaining editorial assistance. The serial, like the slide show, may be viewed as an intermediate step. As the individual articles appear, they may elicit additional information, and once the series is complete the articles can be collected into a book.

Finally, local historians sometimes find teachers in the schools a receptive audience for their work. Information about a local business may help the teacher present a unit in a course of study so as to increase the curriculum's relevance to the students. One of us, while teaching in an urban public school, once used historical materials from a local department store to help middle school students learn about changing gender roles in American society. The materials included a series of advertisements from the past contrasted with contemporary advertisements, and interviews with a few of the store's buyers who had experienced changing customs over the years of their service.

To use the media described above successfully it is necessary to pay careful attention to the collection and interpretation of artifacts and images during the research process. There are pitfalls to avoid. Foremost among the pitfalls is allowing the story to be dictated by the visuals. Images must be used to illustrate the story, not become the story. Another consideration is the need to obtain high-quality photographic copies of images. In using photography, it is important to have good equipment and an understanding of the medium in which you are working.

Conclusion

Exploring the history of a local firm presents exciting possibilities indeed. Throughout the project several different types of presentations are described. At the start of a project, a magazine article may seem like the best approach. Then, as the questions raised open new insights, the project may include expansion of the article into a book. And the research experience may uncover audio and visual materials, and other artifacts, that lend themselves well to media other than print. In the final analysis, the discovery and presentation of business history depends to a great extent on the creativity of the nearby historian.

Suggested Readings

The *Public Historian* 3 (Summer 1981) is devoted to the theme of "Business and History" and contains valuable essays on how historians can present the results of their work to the public.

Index

Illustrations are indicated by **boldface** *numerals.*